PARK LIFE

Urban Parks and Social Renewal

A report by Comedia
in association with Demos

PARK LIFE

Urban Parks and Social Renewal

Contents

First published May 1995
Reprinted August 1995 by

Comedia, The Round, Bournes Green, Stroud, Glos GL6 7NL
Tel: 01452 770624   Fax: 01452 770596
& **Demos**, 9 Bridewell Place, London EC4V 6AP
Tel: 0171 353 4479   Fax: 0171 353 4481

ISBN 1873 667 86 8

Printed by Da Costa Print (London) on chlorine–free paper

ACKNOWLEDGEMENTS

We would like to thank the following organisations and individuals for making available funding for this study, without which it would not have happened. They are **The Baring Foundation** (David Carrington), the **Corporation of London** (Michael Cassidy), the **Economic & Social Research Council**, and the **GMB** (Mick Graham & Phil Woolas).

Thanks are also due to the following members of the Advisory Board who gave their time and expertise, and certainly sharpened up the issues time and again at the Advisory Board meetings: Alan Barber, Franco Bianchini, Mrs Christine MacKenzie Cohen, Robin Grove–White, Susan Lasdun, Doreen Massey, Geoff Mulgan, David Nicholson Lord, Nick Tilley, Tom Turner, Colin Ward and Patrick Wright.

We would particularly like to thank those local authority officers who made up the Steering Group for the study and also undertook the day to day work of co–ordinating the case studies: Jon Wheatley, Michelle Wood and Ian Bayliss (Bristol), Robbie Stoakes, Peter Joyce and Patricia Goodwin (Bromley), John Scrimgeour (Cardiff), Mike Rowan, Howard Simmons & Liz High (Hounslow), Tony Dyckhoff and John Salter (Greenwich), Richard Welburn (Leicester), Robert Hobbs (Merton), Gordon Bates and Mick Hannon (Middlesbrough), Lloyd Snellgrove (Sheffield), Colin Brand (Southwark) and John Fisher & Robin Windsor (Sutton). From the Dublin local authorities we would like to thank Gerard Barry (Dublin Corporation), Dr Christy Boylan (South Dublin County Council), John McCullen (Office of Public Works), Michael Lynch (Fingal County Council) and Denis Shannon (Dun Laoghaire County Council).

For contributing to the series of seminars, we would like to thank Jacquie Burgess, Carolyn Harrison, Mick Hannon, Bob Hughes, Naseem Khan, Andrew Mawson, Geoff Mulgan, Nick Tilley, Wendy Titman, Colin Ward, Michelle Wood and Sandy Wynn.

For administrative support, thanks to Martin Bartle and Joanna Wade at Demos, and Susie Trotter at Comedia. Thanks are also due to Charles Landry, Bob Lumley and John Newton for their invaluable comments on the final draft, to Larraine Worpole for providing photographs for the study, including the one on the cover, and to François Matarasso for lay–out and design.

The report is based on original research undertaken by Peter Boarder, Chris Burton, Liz Greenhalgh, Naseem Khan, François Matarasso, John Newton, Rebecca O'Rourke, Dave Slater, Sue Swingler and Ken Worpole, with support from Yen–Chit Chong & Lia Ghilardi. The project was managed by Liz Greenhalgh & Ken Worpole, who are also responsible for writing the final report.

KEY THEMES & SUMMARY OF REPORT

This report is based on an 18 month research project carried out in partnership with twelve local authorities—Bristol, Bromley, Cardiff, Dublin[1], Greenwich, Hounslow, Leicester, Merton, Middlesbrough, Sheffield, Southwark, Sutton—in the course of which more than 10,000 park users were observed, and more than 1,000 park users interviewed. In addition 12 local case studies were undertaken on specific themes. It is one of the largest surveys of public park use conducted for many years.

THEMES OF THE RESEARCH

The declining quality of Britain's urban parks and open spaces is now a matter of extensive public concern, and is part of a wider fear that we can no longer manage safety and well–being in public spaces. Is the 'keeper–less park', along with the unstaffed railway station, the poorly-lit underground car park, the unsupervised playground, and the deserted town centre at night, going to become another ghost zone of modern Britain? Many people think so, while others look to the new wildlife parks and city farms to provide a different model of urban greenspace. While concentrating on urban parks, this report includes in its definition of urban open spaces a whole range of types—neighbourhood parks, town parks, linear parks, regional parks, commons, cemeteries, school playing fields, children's playgrounds, urban farms, canal paths, beck valleys, allotments, community gardens, urban woodlands, abandoned wasteland, land around the old utilities—and asks how they can be managed in future to add to a new quality of urban life.

Perceived decline

Public parks are one of the most enduring and defining types of public space in Britain's towns and cities, and yet their use and the contribution they make to urban quality of life has been undervalued and taken for granted. In the Victorian era, parks were at the forefront of urban development; today they are often an after–thought, at the bottom of the political agenda.

Bottom of the urban agenda

The research for this study shows that successful parks—and there are still many of them—fulfil many complex urban needs, often in highly sustainable ways. By and large they are local facilities; people who use them, use them frequently; they mostly walk to them; and they are accessible to all ages, and all walks of life. Many people take great pride in 'their' park, and it is often the meeting place and focal point of that elusive notion of 'community'. Few other urban institutions or facilities possess this openness and flexibility. Parks are often a source of local continuity and 'sense of place' in a rapidly changing urban scene.

Sense of place

No commercial alternatives

The report argues that quality of life is as much about the 'taken for granted' world of the urban park—whether it be the children's playground, the local bowls club, somewhere to walk the dog, to go for a family picnic, the informal ball game, somewhere to stroll on a summer's evening, the opportunity to get out of the house for a breath of fresh air and a chance to see grass and trees—as it is about more consumer–based forms of leisure. If the park continues to decline, are the alternative models—theme parks, private sports clubs, regional country parks, indoor sports facilities—credible alternatives? We think not.

A realm of freedom

There is a sense, then, that the world of the park is uniquely a realm of urban freedom, where a different sense of time, of closeness to the elements, to the 'unharmed world', is apparent; and people value this more than is currently realised, though they may find it difficult to express precisely. The park is both a sanctuary, and a place where many people mark the passage of their lives.

Safer parks, safer cities

Yet evidence from interviews and discussion groups shows that the pressing issues of public safety, and the perception of personal safety for oneself and for one's children, are today most symbolised in the decline of the public park. This report strongly favours the argument that the key to safer cities, to safer streets, and to safer parks, is through better management, care and use of the public realm, than it is through greater use of surveillance technology, more intense policing, and an acquiescence in the attitude that in modern towns and cities it is now safer and better to stay indoors.

Managerial conservatism

One of the key conclusions arising from the study is that radical thinking and action are needed if decline is not only to be averted but reversed. A better relationship between central and local government with regard to the funding and management of parks is a priority. The current emphasis on cost–cutting and 'efficiency' through contracting out has led to a general attitude of political and managerial conservatism. Greater flexibility in the ways in which parks and open spaces are funded, managed, and developed to suit changing needs, is also now urgent. There are opportunities for all kinds of new partnerships, and all kinds of new public spaces. The growth and success of city farms, ecology gardens, urban wildlife trusts, newly developed urban public squares and pedestrianised streets, attests to the opportunities for successful renewal.

A strategy for renewal

The strategy this report recommends for reviving many parks and open spaces is long term. It eschews the short–term needs of local and national politicians for 'results', for 'quick–fix' solutions, or for competitive electoral advantage. It is based on the following arguments:

- That not all open space is sacrosanct;

- That there may be many established parks which have lost much of their local resident population and may have to be developed to suit some more modern purpose or set of local needs;

- That it is quite possible to have too much open space in a particular town or city, or too big a park or recreation ground to warrant any local sense of ownership or affection;

- That parks may make ideal settings for the development and siting of new educational, social and cultural facilities—such as nursery schools, educational interpretation centres, ecology centres, arts centres and museums;

- And that the very best will only be achieved by different sectors and interests working together.

The long tradition of the village green, the market square, the public commons, lammas lands, the town square and the Victorian park have all been central to a sense of local identity and belonging. This long line of innovation and renewal now seems exhausted in many places. What will this generation leave future generations in the way of exciting, diverse, rich and sustainable places in our towns and cities, places where they will find a sense of continuity, of relief from the pressures of urban living, places to be in touch with the natural cycles of the seasons, and of wildlife, and also places both to be alone at times but also places to meet and celebrate with others. This is the challenge set by this report.

1	*The Study Brief & Objectives.*
2	*Law, Money & Management,* by Alan Barber.
3	*Lost Childhoods: Taking Children's Play Seriously,* by Bob Hughes.
4	*Calling in the Country: Ecology, Parks and Urban Life,* by David Nicholson Lord.
5	*Parks, Open Space and the Future of Urban Planning,* by Professor Janice Morphet.
6	*Lost Connections and New Directions: the private garden and the public park,* by Martin Hoyles.
7	*Reclaiming the Night: night–time use, lighting and safety in Britain's Parks,* by Carl Gardner (with Jonathan Speirs).
8	*The Politics of Trust: reducing fear of crime in urban parks,* by Jacquie Burgess.
9	*The Popular Culture of City Parks,* by David Crouch.
10	*Age and Order: the public park as a metaphor for a civilized society,* by Dr Hilary A. Taylor.
11	*The Sporting Life: sport, health and active recreation in urban parks,* by Michael F. Collins.
12	*Urban Parks in Germany: Current Issues,* by Ralf Ebert.

WORKING PAPERS

Close reference is made in the report to the 12 Working Papers specially commissioned and published during the course of the study

SUMMARY OF REPORT

Modern Parks
The pleasures
and problems

In Section I, the report examines the close link between the growth of cities during the era of industrialisation and the development of public parks. It looks at the range of open spaces now prevalent in British towns and cities, and questions whether local authorities have developed sufficiently flexible management regimes to cater for this range of diversity. It notes an absence of local and national research into the patterns of use of parks, and whether the parks and open spaces we now have are in the right places and of the right type to meet modern needs.

Cities in Transition

In Section II, the contemporary demographic shifts and changes in cities are noted, particularly where these are relevant to parks and open space provision. Among the most important shifts are the continuing loss of urban populations to the suburbs and, to a lesser extent, the countryside, changes in household composition, and the growing prevalence of home–based, market–provided forms of leisure. Local government planning guidelines are criticised for their emphasis on quantity rather than quality of open space. A continuing and widespread decline in spending on parks is also noted, since savings made through CCT are frequently lost to parks budgets.

Open–minded Spaces

Section III looks at the revival of interest in questions of urban vitality, and in the safety and security of public space. It notes that in modern societies, the 'public' can no longer be seen as an homogenous mass with common needs, but as an overlapping set of groups, communities, lifestyles and interests. Public provision has to adapt to these changing patterns of wants and needs. However, parks have proved highly adaptable to different purposes and different interests, and that is one of their great strengths. In an era in which public and private space is increasingly monitored, surveilled, ordered and controlled, the park represents a realm of freedom, an openness to the elements, and to spontaneity and informal pleasures and contemplation.

The Pressures
for Change

In Section IV, current perceptions and popular representations of parks are examined, particularly the general consensus of neglect, danger and decline. The different approaches and concerns of lobbies and interest groups which have attached themselves to the cause of urban parks are critically examined, whether they be the conservation and heritage groups, the ecology groups, the sports and recreation lobbies, landscaping and urban planning interest, among others. It questions the low status that parks provision now seems to occupy in local authority political culture.

Park Life Today: the
research findings

Section V summarises the large quantitative and qualitative research programme undertaken as part of the study, and in which over 10,000 park users were observed in the summer of 1994, more than 1,200 people interviewed in person, and many discussion groups held. It should be noted that it was a very fine summer, and that the winter use of parks was not reflected in the quantitative research. Of the many findings, it noted that:

- The majority of people tend to visit parks as part of a group;

- About 70% of those interviewed walk to parks;

- The majority take less than five minutes to get to their local park;

- As many as 40% of users interviewed claimed to visit their local park every day;

- The majority of those interviewed would spend about 30 minutes on their visit;

- Most park users claimed to feel safe in their parks in daylight hours;

- Bringing children to parks is the main reason given for atten-dance, with general strolling and dog–walking being the other main reasons;

- A significant number of people claimed never to visit the coun-tryside;

- The majority of people had access to private gardens;

- Access to a car is the most variable factor in the different local surveys;

- There is a slight over–representation of males and an under–representation of the elderly in many of the surveys;

- There is a low level of use by disabled people;

- There is 1 dog for every 8 people on average in a park on any day;

- There appear to be quite particular patterns of use by ethnic minority groups.

In Section VI the report looks at management issues, on the impact of CCT (Compulsory Competitive Tendering), on the development of specific parks strategies by local authorities in the UK, and to the press-ing issues of vandalism, safety, and the restoration of confidence in the public that parks do have a future in modern leisure provision.

A Question of Management

Section VII looks at some lost traditions of public parks, notably the early 19th century tradition of the evening pleasure garden, and later 20th century ideas that parks should become the setting of a wide range of related educational, cultural and recreational provision, inclu-ding kindergartens, health centres, community centres, sports provi-sions, theatres, and so on. It examines the growing importance of the links to be made between parks and urban health and anti–poverty strategies, and looks at the implications for planning. The section con-cludes with an understanding as to how parks issues can be related to Local Agenda 21 strategies in local authorities in the UK.

New Perspectives

Ways Forward   The report concludes with Ways Forward, a programme for action to restore the vitality of urban parks and the contribution they can make to urban and social renewal. It principally recommends that:

- Local authorities should draw up local strategies for parks management and development, including where feasible individual management plans for individual parks;

- There should be a re–formulation of budgets so that expenditure is tied to objectives, including the establishment of investment funds;

- Future budgets should allow for a regular programme of monitoring use of local parks and open spaces;

- Strategy objectives should include a greater pro–active approach to encouraging the use of parks by local communities and to the involvement of local people in the development and management of parks;

- Local policies on safety and security in parks and open spaces should be part of a wider strategy on safety and security in public spaces;

- Local authorities should ensure that policies on parks and open spaces are at the centre of local Agenda 21 policies;

- Urban parks should be placed at the centre of DoE urban regeneration policy;

- The DoE should establish an Urban Parks Unit to disseminate best practice, to develop challenge funding programmes, and provide other central services to benefit local funding, management and development;

- Urban parks should be considered as suitable sites for investment from Lottery funds.

We believe the urban park could once again come into its own as a site for social renewal. In the words of one of the town planners of post–war Britain, all new urban developments should 'Start with the Park!'

MODERN PARKS: THE PLEASURES AND PROBLEMS

Section I

This section provides an overview of the current provision of parks and open spaces, offers some definitions of types, evidence of use, and summarises both the pleasures and the problems of modern parks.

The history of parks and open spaces is inseparable from the develop-   Introduction
ment of the modern town or city. Parks are part of the urban process
and way of life. Many public parks were established in response to the
dramatic growth of the industrial cities in the second half of the last
century, and were emblems of the tensions and values expressed in the
Victorian city: they represented qualities of spaciousness, sunlight,
wholesomeness and health; and were seen as restorative in contrast to
the rapidly developing industrial cities often described as enclosed,
dark, vice–ridden, diseased and corrupting. [2] Cities and parks should
be regarded as inter–dependent. As the dynamics of cities change, so
the use, role and value of public parks change too.

PARKS & PARK USE

What kinds of parks and open spaces are now prevalent in cities, and   A range of spaces
how are they distributed across towns and cities? We would include in
the larger picture, streets, squares, market places as well as neighbourhood parks, town parks, linear parks, regional parks, commons, cemeteries, school playing fields, children's playgrounds, urban farms, canal
paths, beck valleys, allotments, community gardens, urban woodlands,
abandoned wasteland, land around the old utilities (railways and water
boards), and so on. Some of this was intentionally planned of course,
but much also has been inherited, particularly common land or
'lammas lands', where public rights of access are enshrined in ancient
legislation. There is clearly now a wide variety of open spaces in cities.

There is very little evidence at all as to national patterns of park or open   Who uses parks?
space use. However the Audit Commission sponsored a MORI survey
in 1992 which provides the following figures. The survey asked a
sample of the population how many visits they had made within the
past 12 months to parks, playgrounds and open spaces. The results
were as in Table 1 overleaf.

The Audit Commission interpret these findings generally by saying that
30% of the population never use parks, while 45% use them regularly,
and the rest only occasionally. But there are no definitions of spaces or
kinds of use. A use could mean simply walking across a piece of common land to get to the shops. For some this may be a positive experience, for others an additional burden.

TABLE 1		
Source: Audit Commission 1992	1 visit	3%
	2 – 3 visits	8%
	4 – 5 visits	5%
	6 – 10 visits	9%
	10 plus visits	45%
	Don't know	2%
	Never	28%

Some local surveys There have been some local surveys of park use, and a number were collected. There is a high degree of similarity in the findings, confirmed by our own much more extensive research. We looked at research commissioned by councils such as Bedford, Bromley, Middlesbrough, Milton Keynes, Southwark, Sheffield, the London Planning Advisory Committee and the Royal Parks, together with a very interesting user survey of Clissold Park in Hackney, undertaken by park users themselves. In brief, slightly more males than females use parks, but females are more regular users. The Sheffield surveys found that parks were more likely to be used by disadvantaged people compared with other leisure facilities. Most people walk to local parks, and about 40% of existing users claim to visit their local park at least twice–weekly. The majority of visits are to bring children, to go for a stroll, to walk a dog, or where there are particular features such as a good cafe, or an animal enclosure, to visit these. People would like to see more staffing, better toilets, and there is a general apprehension that parks are in decline.

In the wrong place Not surprisingly, open space is very unevenly distributed across towns, boroughs or districts—and in terms of modern needs is often in the wrong place. That is to say it is often not matched to local housing densities or road patterns. Geographical Information Systems (GIS) such as the 'space syntax' programme developed by the Bartlett School of Architecture show the complex way in which particular areas in the urban fabric can become inaccessible and marginalised as the city's road patterns and pedestrian flows are channelled elsewhere.

Not only can parks become marginalised by new street patterns, they also often can be separated from the lives of the streets themselves. As was pointed out in one of the study seminars, while Britain has a strong tradition of public parks, it has a weak tradition, compared to many other European countries, of urban street life: 'the reason the parks in Britain are good is because the quality of the street life is so bad'.

Legacies and liabilities Many urban parks have been formed from historic landed estates, sometimes given to public bodies or purchased by them for public use. Some of these parks came complete with large stately houses, which have been converted for use into changing rooms and cafes, or are now boarded up because of prohibitive maintenance costs. Local authorities therefore often find themselves struggling to manage and maintain great legacies of open spaces and buildings, which in no way fit local patterns of housing, recreation and contemporary demographic change. What was an act of generosity in one generation, may become a liability to the next.

publicans pass the parcel.

Local authorities only own or manage some of these spaces, and within local authorities different departments—Housing, Planning, Leisure Services, Environmental Services—may own and manage them differently. This can lead to public confusion as to the codes of conduct appropriate to each—or even awareness as to who owns or manages them. The codes of behaviour most appropriate to an ornamental garden will differ from those of a children's playground, a cemetery, an allotment, a piece of scrubland or a roadside verge. Arguments over dog mess, loud radios, teenage hanging out, scramble bikes, free festivals, all contribute to the problem of a confusion of appropriate activities for appropriate spaces. In a recent American report on parks, *The Once and Future Park*, Deborah Karasov has identified exactly the same problem:

Appropriate behaviour

> 'Further complicating the picture is that our expectations for public life have also changed greatly since the prototypical parks were created. While some park users stroll along the paths and sit quietly among the manicured gardens—the image of bourgeois leisure to which nineteenth–century reformers hoped everyone would aspire —others feel just as comfortable using parks as places to fix their cars, dance to music, or just hang out. That some feel such behaviour is misbehaviour reflects a deficiency in the variety of parks we have today and in the way parks designers have thought about them.' [3]

A lot of public space may appear to have no management philosophy at all. For example, many current 'estates action' refurbishment schemes pay little or no attention to the management of the (often critical) open spaces in and around housing estates, which then become a kind of no–man's–land or gang turf or territory. The Merton case study was essentially about proposing new uses, designs, activities and management processes for a piece of common land at the centre of a large housing estate undergoing a major refurbishment programme.

PLEASURES

All of this typological confusion, and in some places increasing formlessness and attenuation of open space, should not be allowed to detract from the fact that many parks and open spaces are still places of enormous pleasure to people; are deeply loved and enjoyed; are greatly used and valued; and provide a focal point and rich source of spatial identity to the neighbourhoods and districts within which they are located. '*Our park is the making of our area*', said one man living near Victoria

A lifeline to another world

Park, Bristol. '*We're blessed with some good parks*', said an elderly woman in Middlesbrough.

> *'It gives you a sense of being away from the city–a sense of openness.'*
> (Man, Bristol)
>
> *'I like the trees, I like the greenery and nature. If you take away all the greenery, what will you have left?'* (Elderly West Indian man, Leicester)
>
> *'We take visitors to show it to them. Anybody who comes to our houses, we go to the park with them. They love it, they really like the animals.'*
> (Teenager, Middlesbrough)

Comments like these were recorded in every one of the towns and cities studied. For regular park users, 'their' local park is a lifeline to another kind of world, of fresh air, trees, greenery, play facilities for children, ponds, birds & animals, friendship, and that illusive sense of 'community'.

Events in parks Many parks are also used for events. In 1994 we noted events ranging from a very local activity such as a 'Bird Box Update' in Dulwich Park in May 1994 (22 children with 4 parents and a teacher, '*a good day had by all*'), an Irish Festival at Peckham Rye (15,000 people); a Handicapped Children's Fete in Victoria Park, Cardiff (1,500); Roath Park Centenary Celebrations, Cardiff (75,000); May Day Festival in Lampton Park, Hounslow (50,000); Open Air Theatre Season, Cannizaro Park, Merton (12,000); Anti–Racist Festival on Plumstead Common (20,000); Summer Arts Festival in Merton Parks (25,000); Hindu Prayer Meeting in Abbey Park, Leicester (20,000 people); International Kite Festival, Ashton Court Estate, Bristol (100,000); Bromley Lions Festival in Norman Park, Bromley (15,000); Beighton Guide Fair, Reignhead Farm, Sheffield (1,500); Sheffield Show, Graves Park (90,000); Youth Challenge Day, Pallister Park, Middlesbrough (2,000); Family Fun Day to mark UN International Year of the Family, Abbey Park, Leicester (10,000), and literally thousands of other events and festivals ranging from guided walks, school sports days, disabled activities, charity galas, ethnic minority fairs, religious revival meetings, BBC Radio 1 Road-shows, political rallies, tree–planting days and so on. The events calendars for parks organised by many local authorities often match their events programmes for building based cultural and sports events, though these obviously take place mostly in the summer months.

Flexibility Unlike many purpose–built buildings—sports halls, swimming pools, opera houses, concert halls, theatres—parks provide an accessible and flexible space for thousands of community events throughout Britain. For example, in Clissold Park, Hackney in the summer of 1994, one weekend saw a Homeless Festival attended by more than 20,000 people, yet shortly after the same park was used for a large Afro–Caribbean Sports Day which attracted more than 10,000 competitors and spectators. Parks are important for ethnic minorities because they allow them to make a public statement of a positive cultural identity, as with the Leeds West Indian Carnival in Roundhay Park, Apna Arts Asian/Milton Meades arts festival in Nottingham's University Park, and *melas* in Newham, Bradford, Greenwich and other places. The flexibility of the urban park allows it be used for all kinds of events throughout the year, thus making it one of the key cultural locations in any town, city or local community, although, of course, such events can be adversely affected by bad weather.

This description of the park as a social meeting place is, however, only one aspect of its unique role in local life. For many people it is an oasis of calm in an otherwise busy and noisy city.

Solitude and sanctuary

> *'I like to go to the park to read, I like to sit in the park and see what's going on without having to be part of it.'* (Teenage girl, Greenwich)
>
> *'I love to go to the park and lie on the grass until I am ready to go home.'* (Woman, Leicester)
>
> *'You can get fresh air in your own garden, but you tend to think of things to do back in the house. In the park you can relax.'* (Man, Hounslow)

All of the researchers who undertook the local park observation exercises and interviews were often astonished at the emotional loyalty expressed by many people to their local park, an attachment which David Crouch argues in his Working Paper also extends to often quite untidy and unmanaged spaces.

The well maintained town centre park can still function in much the same way as the Victorian park used to: it commonly is a prestige park, it has a large catchment area, a high profile, good facilities and is designed for intensive use, but the roles for other kinds of parks are more ambiguous and tied to the future development of cities. A good park can raise the value of the housing immediately surrounding it, as many estate agents will testify. On the other hand, a neglected or vandalised park can detract from the value of the neighbourhood; as one of our respondents said, *'why do people say that when you live by the park, the price of your house comes down?'*

The town park

PROBLEMS

Successful parks are the tip of the iceberg. For every well managed, well supported park, there are many other open spaces which the public feel to be in decline or empty and bleak. There appear to be problems of public drinking, or policies of 'care in the community' which make some parks a bolt–hole for the mentally ill. In some places, we were told, the police move those whom they regard as 'undesirables' into the park to keep them off the streets and out of the public eye.

Tip of the iceberg

Vandalism There are clear problems of vandalism too, which also tends to indicate loss of esteem, ownership and local loyalty. The report by The Garden History Society and The Victorian Society, *Public Prospects: Historic Urban Parks Under Threat*, by Hazel Conway & David Lambert (1993) details distressing incidents of vandalism in parks around the country, including the severe damaging of the 1872 memorial fountain in Kelvingrove Park, restored in 1988 at a cost of £158,000 and once again now boarded up; the arson of the boathouse in Dartmouth Park, West Bromwich, again only recently restored at great cost, and many others. The local authorities participating in this study all report cases of vandalism, often minor, such as graffiti, or broken swings, sometimes major, such as in the burning down of bowling pavilions, bandstands or depot buildings. The idea that vandalism is only caused by the young was contradicted by several local authorities who said that in their experience vandalism had on occasions been caused by older people, often men in their thirties. Dog–walkers have also been known to deliberately walk through new planting, and even break down fences, to carry out their regular walk.

Vandalism & Repair – A vicious circle

> *'A lot of it is to do with the local people as well, people do dump things in the stream. But I think if it's shown to be neglected, nobody will respect it. They say we abuse it, and we say they don't maintain it. I don't know how you break that.'*
> **Killinarden Resident, Dublin**

Dog mess Some parks and open spaces are now almost exclusively used by dog-owners to exercise their pets, and are little more than animal toilets. On the other hand it is clear that dog–owners are among the heaviest and most sociable of park users in many places, and are often the 'eyes and ears' of the park. Yet there appears to be a critical point at which a green open space is deserted by anybody other than dog–owners on health and amenity grounds.

For many people, dog mess is the issue symbolising park decline, and from time to time there is a national outcry about it. From this study it is clear that there is no one simple, single solution. A reliance on securing parliamentary approval for new local by–laws is time consuming, and where they exist, often remain ineffective. Passing laws that cannot be enforced makes a nonsense of them. Banning dogs from parks would mean banning a significant proportion of the park users, many of whom are active in park and community affairs, and are responsible dog owners. Poop–scoop schemes, dog–areas, dog–free zones, all help, but in the end it is a hearts and minds job. The most successful local campaigns have been well thought out in advance, widely publicised, working through schools and community groups, consistent and with a long time scale—and effectively enforced. One–off campaigns, moralising campaigns which are not consistently backed up by supervision, largely fail. Attitudes can change—for example with regard to drinking and driving, or smoking in public places—but these require national and local campaigning, backed up by consistent enforcement.

There is a very common kind of green open space, often designated as a playing field, sports field or recreation ground, which is often little used, apparently unloved, and avoided by most people in the community. At their worst, such flat, levelled green sites—which possess no ecological, aesthetic or general amenity value—are perhaps used for the occasional Saturday match or some mid–week kickaround, although at their best they do provide places for organised games. We were told by a parks manager whose office overlooked such a playing field, that in winter when the pitches were marked out and the goal posts installed, the occasional woman or elderly walker using the field as a through–route would walk round the edges of the pitches which were regarded as forbidden territory, even though it was a much longer route. In such ways certain kinds of open space are deeply territorialised.

'Geographies of rejection'

'In a nutshell, our urban parks are in crisis. They are obsolete in terms of design, often badly managed and to an increasing extent are being ignored by their public. They are expensive to keep in terms of the return they provide. I know of no park anywhere in this country which is designed, or has been re-designed to meet the contemporary needs of the people able to use it.'

Brian Clouston, Landscape Design, June 1984

The question of people's fears about safety in public spaces is dealt with at much greater length later in this report, but it is germane at this point to signal the issue that it is precisely people's fears about safety and security for themselves, their children and loved ones in parks and open spaces that continues to dominate most people's criticisms of what is currently least attractive about current parks management. '*Why would I want to go to a park on my own,*' asked a young woman incredulously in a discussion group in Leicester. '*I'm not a nervous person, but I just don't feel very safe in the park now,*' said an elderly woman in Middlesbrough. '*That's the way we're treated, you know. There's no security people in the park, nobody supervising the children. They fight and swear, nobody minds if they're fighting and swearing at us, you know,*' said an Asian woman, one of a discussion group in Middlesbrough. One elderly Asian man in Hounslow described going to the park very early in the morning '*when these muggers are sleeping*'. On an outlying estate in Dublin, a local resident said that, '*the park is known in the area as a place to avoid, even during the day you feel unsafe up there. Children are unsafe, and won't go up alone*'.

Places of fear

Too many green open spaces simply look the same and no longer possess any distinguishing or distinctive features, if they ever did. Their layout has gradually been adapted to suit the convenience of the tractors and mowers used in cutting the grass; in short the park has been designed for the mower, rather than the mower for the park. This has been compounded by the increasing pressure to cut management

Parks fit for mowing machines

and maintenance costs. They are mass produced sites and are maintained as such.

Cemetery Manager 'Often the simplest programmes of gang–mowing are preferred, since they are easiest to write into the specification. The structure of local authority cemetery management, therefore, offers little opportunity to implement conservation programmes, which need to be tailored to specific sites, and even particular zones within sites.'[4]

How are they managed? The study therefore raises quite fundamental questions about the capacity of local authorities to manage the infrastructure that they have inherited, given all the political, managerial and financial constraints within which they now operate. The difficult questions as to whether some places actually have too much open space, a lot of which is perceived to be uninviting, even dangerous, and poorly maintained, or in the wrong place, are still being avoided. There is an urgent need for a new rationale for the provision of public open space, which involves questions of ownership, management and potential new sources of funding. These themes are referred to again and again throughout the report, and if there is repetition it is because there are no easy answers —but the questions will still not go away.

CITIES IN TRANSITION   **Section II**

This section summarises the evidence to show ways in which cities are changing, with the population drift away from cities, the clustering of ethnic minorities communities in a limited number of urban areas, changing household composition, and other demographic impacts on urban life. All these structural changes are bound to have an influence on parks and park use.

DEMOGRAPHIC CHANGE

The main changes in cities occurring in the last quarter of the 20th century are: the decline in manufacturing industry; continued suburbanisation; continued technological change; and changes in lifestyle preferences. These shifts are not superficial details but stand to alter the deeper structure of cities. 'They are creating new, more dispersed forms of urban settlement in which our old concepts of the city have less and less relevance, and in which the urban fringe is becoming the new centre of activity,' argues Philip Kivell.[5] Indeed, another policy analyst, William Solesbury, points out that in some places de-industrialisation has produced vast tracts of vacant and derelict land, and that these wastelands are on a scale not hitherto seen in urban development.[6]

Changing structure of cities

However, policies have been carried through to improve city centres, and to try to strengthen the pull of the city centre. More recently government has shown concern about prolonged out of town development and has stated a wish to curb out of town growth. The lower density suburban style house building and activities such as recreation, airports, waste disposal are also spreading outside the city boundaries. There is a debate to be had about the future of cities. For example Janice Morphet in Working Paper 5 argues that compact cities in which collective services can be provided are more sustainable, while others, such as David Nicholson Lord in Working Paper 4, argue that the trend is now irreversibly towards more dispersed settlement form and that in the longer term smaller centres are more adaptable to renewable forms of energy.

Compact or dispersed ?

Britain's population is still concentrated in urban areas. In England and Wales, 89% of the population live in urban areas on 7.7 per cent of the land. [7] Nevertheless despite the high concentration of populations in urban systems, the last few decades have witnessed a decentralisation of population. The 11 case–study areas all show population decline between 1961 and 1991.

Demographic change

TABLE 2

Population present on census night: 1961–91

(Leicester & Cardiff have had boundary changes since 1981. Note also the 1974 Local Government re–organisation)

Source: OPCS 1991 Census Historical Tables Great Britain.

	1961	1991
Bristol	438,038	370,300
Bromley	293,394	281,700
Cardiff	289,862	272,600
Greenwich	229,810	200,800
Hounslow	208,893	193,400
Leicester	288,039	270,600
Merton	189,013	161,800
Middlesbrough	164,762	141,100
Sheffield	584,806	499,700
Southwark	313,413	196,500
Sutton	169,095	164,300

Centre to periphery Whilst these city or borough populations have declined (some more than others) other surrounding areas or districts have increased in population size. Bristol has declined while North Avon for example has grown. Sheffield has shown a decrease while Doncaster and Rotherham in South Yorkshire show a slight increase. Cardiff shows a decrease, while the Vale of Glamorgan returns an increase. Middlesbrough shows a decrease while Langbaugh–on–Tees and Stockton show increases. Dublin has undergone a major shift of population from the city centre to new towns on the periphery in the last twenty years. The figures for London are:

TABLE 2

All three areas have had boundary changes since 1961

	1961	1991
Greater London	7,992,616	6,377,900
Outer Met area	4,344,824	5,418,700
Outer South East	3,656,248	4,917,100

This supports the pattern of 'fringe' development.

Re–urbanisation In contrast during the 1980s, re–urbanisation began to emerge elsewhere in Europe. In Germany, France and Holland, several large and medium sized towns grew in population.[8] A study by Liverpool John Moores University suggests that demographic trends reflect economic trends and the economic recovery in the case of the growth of Hamburg, Rotterdam and Amsterdam. Recent research in Britain also suggests that in some cities, population is beginning to grow again.

Household composition Changing household composition has had a major effect on the structure of cities, and therefore on the use of city parks. Research shows that the main demographic impact upon land use in many cities has not come from population growth, but rather from its re–structuring, as a result of ageing, divorce and a decrease in shared accommodation. 'The population of Great Britain grew by just 0.57% between 1971 and 1981, but the number of households grew by 7.4%. This reflects a fall in average household size from 2.88 to 2.71 persons'. Fewer people in each dwelling and a decrease in the typical densities for housing has meant increased pressure for housing.[9] A study of household change in the 1980s for Population Trends states that the 1980s saw the most rapid decline in household size in the past half century. The study identified an increase in the proportion of young adults living alone, sharing with others, and remaining at home with parents with a corresponding reduction in those living as couples with children. These patterns were found to be more marked for women than men. The other area of significant change in living arrangements was found among the older elderly who are now more likely to be living independently.[10]

A recent study in *Population Trends*[11] shows that ethnic minority populations tend to live in a relatively small number of urban areas. Even within those areas ethnic populations tend to be concentrated within a very few wards of a city. The analysis demonstrates a marked spatial segregation in the location of ethnic groups, and points to the isolation of ethnic minority groups within small areas of cities. Ethnic minority use of parks often takes distinct forms and patterns as this study shows.

Ethnic minority populations

LEISURE AND LIFESTYLES

The world for which the Victorian park was developed has changed beyond recognition. Failure to acknowledge or respond to these changes is part of the problem. Among the most important we might note the following:

The world we have lost

The CPRE report 'Leisure Landscapes' states that more than 70% of UK households possess a car, and that there has been a doubling of passenger mileage every two decades since 1945. 45% of all car journeys are now made for leisure purposes and this proportion of car use is expected to increase faster than for other sectors. One of the results of increasing car ownership, and the success of the Countryside Commission in promoting the growth of country parks in the 1980s has been that the park, like the shopping centre, has gone 'out of town'. For those that can afford it, the Sunday stroll in the local park has been replaced by the car–based trip to the country park, where visitors are likely to find car parking, toilets, interpretation centres, activities, gift shops and a more structured 'experience'.

Car ownership

> *'The parks have gone out of fashion now, because you've got your theme parks, and people want different things from parks now.'*

Woman Interviewee, Leicester

Households without access to a car are often concentrated in particular localities, so that there may well be areas where up to 50% of households do not have access to a car, as we found in parts of Greenwich, Sutton, Sheffield and Southwark.

Increase in private gardens

When parks were 'invented' in response to 19th century urban conditions, the majority of the population were unlikely to have had access to a garden, or perhaps even a yard. For the experience of horticultural excellence they flocked to the park. Today, however, it is claimed that some 85% of all households have access to a garden. Domestic gardening is now a £2bn industry supported by a wide range of specialist magazines and TV programmes, as Martin Hoyles has pointed out in Working Paper 6. Sunday visits to garden centres, usually located on edge of town sites, are now a popular alternative to visiting the local park. The link between the private garden and the public park has in many ways been broken, and local authorities have failed to renew the relationship.

Home–based entertainment

Over the last 30 years there has been a growth in home entertainment, TV, video, satellite, music. In some ways the world of leisure has moved from the outdoors to the indoors, from the street to the living room, although there are plenty of leisure trends—percentage of the population eating out, car trips, walking statistics—which also exhibit reverse patterns.

'Not allowed out...'

Of particular relevance to the context for modern park use, has been research showing the loss of children's independence and mobility in the modern city. Statistics taken from Mayer Hillman's seminal report, *Children, Transport and the Quality of Life*, show that:

- Three–quarters of children aged between 7 & 11 were allowed to cross roads on their own in 1971, compared to just half in 1991;

- Half were allowed to use buses on their own in 1971, compared to only 1 in 7 in 1991;

- Nearly four times as many children were chauffeured to school in 1991 as in 1971;

- 90% of children in the UK own a bicycle but only 1 in 25 trips are made by bicycle. In the Netherlands the ratio is 2 in 3.[12]

Extended living room

A study by John Moores University notes the recent increase in single person households in some city centres, against the general post–war exodus. This can often be seen as part of a process of gentrification, but it also reflects improved living, working, social and cultural facilities in some city centres. Recent research in Amsterdam showed very high percentages of one person households in the city centre and that people from these households are users of the city centre's recreational facilities. 'The choice to live alone does not imply a choice to be alone. To meet other people these people need to go out far more often than the traditional family households. One could say that these modern households use the city centre as an extension of their living room'.[13] For such city–dwellers the park may become their garden—a place for sun–bathing, picnics and other social occasions.

THE PLANNING LEGACY

As the population moves, the older 19th century parks once used by a high density inner city population, are often left almost stranded, with fewer houses, fewer work places and new neighbouring areas of derelict land. This has certainly happened to some parks in Manchester and Liverpool. Phillips Park in Manchester, once a highly popular and greatly loved park, has now been left isolated as the residential population surrounding it has been moved on. The park has been marginalised by the new road system and disregarded in the adjacent development of new leisure facilities.

The park in the city

In planning terms, problems of typology clearly continue to thwart the development of strategic park policies in many places. Hitherto so much thinking about open space has concentrated on quantity—so many hectares, so much open space per head of population. The fact is, some parks can be too big for their own good. A Dublin resident described Hartstown Park as '*an asset to the community, but it's too big. Too much space and nothing done in the space*'.

Quantity not quality

Therefore questions of quality are now the order of the day, and it is important to shift the strategic arguments about parks and open spaces from crude statistical approaches, to more specialist, needs–based approaches.

A starting point for open space planning in post–war Britain was the highly influential 1943 Abercrombie Plan which proposed 4 acres per 1,000 population. This was regarded as a basis for growth. The GLC in its Greater London Development Plan, which has informed many London UDP's, proposed an Open Space Hierarchy typology of 4 categories, all based on size: Metropolitan (150 acres within 2 miles reach), District (50 acres within 3/4 miles reach), Local (5 acres within 1/4 mile reach) and Small Local (under 5 acres). The 1993 London Planning Advisory Committee study on London parks suggested adding Regional Parks and Linear Parks to this Hierarchy. But this report by Llewellyn Davies also suggested adding qualitative attributes such as Hilly Topography, Undulating Topography, Variety of Different Spaces, Ornamental Layout, Attractive Views Beyond Park, as well as positive features such as Streams, Lakes, Architectural Features, Quiet, Winter Flowering Shrubs, Sense of Safety.

Tom Turner's report for the Landscape Institute publication on urban parks (1992), stated that 'The Unitary Development Plans make little or no attempt to deal with the historic lack of conceptual precision (with regard to open space types), or with the serious theoretical criticism to which the concepts have been subject.' What is true of London is also true of many other British towns and cities—planning has not yet developed ways of thinking anew about the open spaces modern cities need.

More open space than ever?

Local authorities maintain about 300,000 acres of urban parks and open spaces in England & Wales. Between 10% and 15% of the total developed area of England and Wales is urban open space, and local authorities spend on average £16 per resident on parks and green spaces. (Audit Commission 1988). The study carried out by the Planning Exchange for the Glasgow Development Agency and Glasgow City Council concludes that most of the 37 international cities reviewed appeared to be adding to the area of park land and open space. In the case of most British cities the National Playing Fields Association standard of 2.43 hectares (six acres) per thousand population has been comfortably exceeded. The study carried out by Llewellyn Davies for LPAC also concluded that the majority of London boroughs had added to their open space over the last 20 years. Work carried out by Tom Turner also for LPAC has shown slight increases in the amount of open space in urban areas.

Budgets &Land Portfolios

The provision, maintenance and management of parks and open spaces remains a significant element in the services which local authorities provide to their populations. For example, Bristol Leisure Services Department manages some 3,900 acres, including 71 parks, 19 open spaces, 3 estates and 7,000 allotments spread over 150 sites. Bromley Council manages 105 sites of council–owned space covering 2,600 acres. Sheffield City Council manages over 5,000 acres of open space including 66 allotment sites, 70 woodlands and 100 playgrounds. Southwark Council, one of London's smallest inner city boroughs, manages more than 120 parks and open spaces comprising 550 acres. Merton Council is responsible for a total of 808 acres of parks and open spaces, plus 440 acres of commons, excluding cemeteries and allotments. In 1994/5, Merton spent £3.48 million net on parks and open spaces, out of a Leisure budget of £7.36 million. Sutton Council manages 1,002 acres, including 51 parks, on a budget of £2.7 million, excluding allotments. Greenwich Council spent £4.4 million on Parks & Cemeteries in 1992/93 involving 1,200 acres (excluding woodland) with a population of 200,000. Comparisons between local authorities are difficult to make because of different departmental responsibilities and allocation of costs.

Spending in decline

The Planning Exchange report to Glasgow City Council and the Development Agency concludes that in most cities expenditure on parks and open space has remained static or is declining. The proportion of total local authority expenditure on parks and open space in the UK ranged from 1.6% in Leeds to 16.5% in Aberdeen.

In summary, the position common to many local authorities is that they are now responsible for a large number of open spaces, which have through management practices tended to lose their distinctiveness; budgets on the whole have declined; parks provision has lost status within the wider leisure field; and some local authorities are now wondering aloud how they can continue to manage the infrastructure of open space, other than by simply overseeing a process of continuing decline.

Many urban theorists, notably Kevin Lynch, have criticised planners and providers for the sheer limitation of types of open space available in cities and the lack of variety of management regimes. Perhaps the greatest criticism to date of parks typologies is that the public simply do not understand them. This has been a theme of current strategic thinking in Bromley: the disparity between how the public understand and value parks and the ways in which local authority planners and parks managers understand and value them. It is also at the heart of the Middlesbrough case study: that the public understand, speak, value and enjoy parks in ways which are often insufficiently understood, monitored or absorbed in official strategies.

Lack of variety

'The first thing to consider is perhaps fairly obvious. What is it being used for? You may think you know but different people see different things. Local residents, casual users, visitors or the Council make assumptions from differing points of view about how they use, appreciate or manage a piece of land. The kids may play games on it, people will walk over it, the Council will cut the grass and perhaps everyone will assume that piece of land is like all the others they know, just there for however they want to enjoy it. Well, practically speaking, it probably is, within reason, that is until the Council want to use it for something else, then you need to look at how you came by it, what powers you hold it under, if you are getting income from it where that money is going, if you are spending money on it where that money comes from, who really uses it, how regularly and why, what's under it or over it, why nobody thought of using this handy piece of land for something else before now?'

Bedford Parks and Green Space: A Position Statement, April 1993

yes!

Mapping, auditing, defining purpose and monitoring use—these are now the urgent pre–conditions for renewal.

Section III OPEN–MINDED SPACES

Questions of safety in public places are now key issues on the urban agenda. This section looks at current debates about safety and security in public spaces, over–regimented traditions of town planning, and suggests that the public park retains some vestiges of natural rights and a sense of freedom, which may be disappearing fast in the highly commercialised and regulated environments of consumer society and urban centres.

Viability & vitality The concern over the effects of zoning, out of town development, ghettos and enclaves, and dead town centres in our towns and cities is now familiar and widely accepted. The DoE has recently issued new planning guidelines with the aim of helping planning authorities to re-interpret their town centres as social places and to help to engender the viability and vitality of town centres.[14] West Park in Wolverhampton is a central feature of the city centre regeneration strategy currently being developed by the council. In Hounslow the improvement of Lampton Park and Inwood Park are seen as being an enhancement to the quality of the town centre, and directly related to the overall town centre regeneration strategy.

Open–minded spaces In his 1995 Reith Lectures, Sir Richard Rogers began by talking about the quality of public spaces as being as important as the buildings they connect. The renewed interest in the state of the public areas of cities reveals deeper concerns about the way cities are developing, and these go beyond the problem of dead town centres and touch upon fundamental questions about the meaning of citizenship and the longer term ecological impact of current urban trends. Rogers has begun to articulate the value of the public realm as places where individuals get a sense of taking part, of communality and of citizenship.[15] He has also made the useful distinction between 'single–minded spaces' of mono-functional planning and more 'open–minded spaces' such as parks which, he claims, 'bring diverse sections of society together, and breed a sense of toleration, identity and mutual respect'.

It is this sense of civil society that Rogers argues has been damaged by the planning and development trends of the last three decades. The opportunity to let people define, develop and manage public areas is an opportunity to encourage new kinds of participation and more radical notions of what decision–making might involve. 'Teaching children about biology and history, but not about their actual environment—the built one—leaves them ill–equipped to participate in the process of respecting and improving the city that so critically affects their lives. We must teach citizenship and listen to citizens'.[16]

Many publics The phrase 'the public realm' is difficult as it refers both to a physical place or space and to a political construction of people as a 'general public'. The idea that a unified public exists (or ever existed), has been challenged. Modern societies are now made up of many different groups with different cultural traditions, beliefs and lifestyles that may at times compete and conflict with each other as much as they find common purposes. Public spaces are not equally available at all times to all people. Certain groups may be effectively excluded or their access can be dependent on time of day. For example, the Comedia survey work showed that young people's use of parks is often not recognised by parks managers because their use is often evening use. In contrast, the majority of day–time park users thought it unlikely they would consider walking in the park in the evenings or after dark. The Royal Parks survey showed that women hardly used parks early in the morning and last thing at night before closing, but were heavily represented during the day. Dog–walkers are very fixed in their 'first thing in the morning, last thing at night' routines. The Comedia observation exercises showed that ethnic minority families would often come to the park only on Sunday afternoons, believing that numbers implied greater safety. The realisation of an increasingly complex and hetero-geneous mix of urban populations implies an ever greater need for well managed public space.

For one recent writer, the key to understanding urban life is an ac-   **Relating to strangers**
knowledgement that to live in cities is to live in a world of strangers. This means that dealing with anonymity is a feature of daily life. An-other argues that we relate to strangers by picking up clues about them from their appearance or from their location.[17] Total anonymity would be unbearable and the places where we see other people help us to understand and anticipate their actions. This is why public settings are important, in that they help us to make sense and understand the pres-ence of others. Parks have always provided settings for informal encounters.

The breakdown in trust between strangers in public places suggests that our ability to anticipate other people's behaviour has been weak-ened and, as Jacquie Burgess describes in her Working Paper, while the public parks in many areas have been very visibly declining, commer-cial shopping centres have made the appearance of a safe and secure environment a high priority. The controlled environment is a very de-liberate facet of the strategy for attracting shoppers. The closed in plazas with high levels of security and high standards of cleaning and maintenance create a safe–zone, an area that is designed to contrast with the shabbier public areas outside. Jacquie Burgess describes the uncertainties and the distrust between strangers that is now common-place in urban Britain and argues that in the case of public parks, fear of crime and victimisation, combined with the withdrawal of person-nel from parks is making the negotiation of access to the park much more difficult.

Safer Cities? Personal safety in modern cities is now a major political issue, and many 'quality of life' studies show that urban success depends on ensuring this better sense of public safety. There is much research to show that women are deterred from using public space through fear of crime, and that the majority of children no longer have the freedom of the streets they once enjoyed. The household surveys carried out in the Cardiff and Southwark case–studies show that, perhaps surprisingly, men slightly more than women fear for their safety in parks. Parks therefore need to become testing grounds for new kinds of safety measures in and around public open space.

The task, as Jacquie Burgess sees it, is to find ways of building a sense of public trust by developing social strategies for reducing fear. By this she means attracting people into parks and managing them in ways that reflect the rights of different groups to be in the parks.[18]

The same point is made by the American environmental design theorist Kevin Lynch. He argues for parks that reflect the complexities of modern social life and the range of social groups in society. The solutions he suggests include giving greater thought to the management of time and space, with the provision of subtle markers that allow each using group to find their place.[19] This sense of creating 'publics' has always been a function of the public park.

Parks make people The Victorian public parks were built to help shape not only the physical structure of the expanding 19th century industrial city, but also the rapidly growing urban population. Public parks were places in which the new populations of the city could see themselves, they helped to give sense to the idea of an urban public. As Hilary Taylor argues in Working Paper 10, the public park was a metaphor for a notion of the civilized society. 'There is absolutely no doubt, too, that these parks were seen as a means of 'civilizing' and cementing a society which was viewed as threateningly unstable in its diversity and explosive growth'. Hilary Taylor describes the detailed planning that went into Victorian parks and the ways in which the design of walkways, formal avenues and sports areas were intended to foster behaviour considered appropriate to urban life. She points out the way nature was introduced into the cities via the parks, and argues that it was not a wild or rustic form of nature, but an image of nature drawn from the guiding philosophies of the age. Park design reflected a spectacle of nature managed and understood, a revelation of 'man's mastery over chaos' and an indication of his evolutionary success. It was an exhibition of nature that enlarged the urban experience; it did not challenge it. The Victorian park also represented ideas about art and culture as much as they represented nature. The formal park or garden is also as much a part of the Asian cultural tradition, deriving from the old Mughal patterns of gardens, and the latter day imperial parks developed under the Raj.

The park was intended as a site for expressing artistic ideals. These ideals were to educate, civilize and ennoble. Park designs drew on influences from classicism, from Japanese traditions and were places for 'the expression of an extrovert confidence, bred of imperial power, for adventure and romance, for vicarious travel and excitement. Hence the Swiss Bridge at Birkenhead; exotic Moorish tracery on a cast–iron shelter at Lincoln Arboretum, and, of course on many a bandstand; the 'Kyber Pass', created in miniature out of artificial stone, at East Park Hull'. Contemporary debates in horticulture and colour displays were bound up with the emerging science of colour theory and the influences informing Pre–Raphaelite, Impressionist and Post Impressionist painting.[20]

The Victorian ambitions for ennobling, educating and creating a respectable urban public through the provision of public parks also involved squashing some of the earlier uses and traditions of open space. Parks were sometimes provided in compensation for the enclosure of common land, places where large crowds could gather and express political demands. They also replaced the pleasure gardens and more informal unregulated uses of open space such as Battersea Fields. As Kevin Lynch noted, Battersea Park was built to provide 'wholesome recreation' in place of the rowdy joys of Battersea Field, once described by The City Mission magazine in September 1870 thus: 'Surely if ever there was a place out of hell that surpassed Sodom and Gomorrah in ungodliness and abomination this was it ...horses and donkeys racing, footracing, walking matches, flying boats, flying horses, roundabouts, theatres, comic actors, shameless dancers, conjurers, fortune tellers, gamblers of every description, drinking booths, stalls, hawkers, and vendors of all kinds of articles...' [21] (As Kevin Lynch commented, what was condemned here in 1870 reads like a blueprint for urban renewal today.)

Pleasure or respectability?

yep!

The use of parks for political meetings and demonstrations has also been a part of their historic function. Indeed, Victoria Park in the east end of London was often described as 'the people's parliament'. William Morris often lectured in the open air, as did many other speakers from different political and religious sects. It was also the regular assembly point for trade union meetings and, more recently, was the place where more than 100,000 people turned up for the first of the major Rock against Racism events in the early 1980s. Bristol parks have also been meeting places for social movements such as the Chartists, trades unions, and various political and religious groups.

On a more utilitarian level, the construction of the Victorian public parks can be seen as part of the rational response to the expansion of cities in the 19th century. They were linked to questions of public health, in fact they can be seen as part of the invention of the idea of 'public health'. The arguments made by the public health movement referred to public parks as part of the solution to the problems of poor

Rationalist planning

public health and the need to control the process of urbanisation. The 1848 Public Health Act provided for the creation of General Boards of Health and allowed local authorities to implement a basic range of sanitary services and minimum physical housing standards. The need to control these burgeoning processes of urbanisation led to state intervention and the creation of the Town Planning Act in 1909. Since then there have been successive waves of park creation, overwhelmingly informed by quantitative rather than qualitative principles. Yet many redevelopment schemes in cities—and of their parks—have happened with little consultation, leaving communities in a radically different environment over which they feel they have no control.

Creating realities In her book on women and planning, Clara Greed argues that planning is not really about saving society from disasters or problem solving, it is about creating realities. Under the 1909 and 1919 Housing and Town Planning Acts local authorities were required to prepare town plans. The town planning approach was based on ideas about housing controls, notions of the correct population density, and zoning—separating work, people and place. It was these themes of ordering and separating functions of urban living in the city that shaped both the Victorian city and the town planning profession.

Much recent writing about cities laments the 'privatisation' of urban public space, but Clara Greed argues that the conceptualisation of many founding fathers of the modern town planning profession favoured public space over private space, and the sense that public space had to be kept separate from the trivia of domesticity and family life within the private realm. She cites the land given over to sports in the post war period and contrasts this with the way in which the standard size of council houses became smaller. She refers to the National Playing Fields Association's success in the inter–war period in recommending 6 acres of playing fields per thousand population, and points out that to create this standard women were included numerically, to support the need for spaces they were unlikely to be welcomed to use.

> The geographer Doreen Massey in her book *Space, Place and Gender* (1994) remembers as a 10 year old on the bus into Manchester passing acres of dank, muddy fields of football and rugby pitches. 'And I remember, too, it striking me very clearly...that all this huge stretch of the Mersey flood plain had been entirely given over to boys.' [22]

Clara Greed is most critical of the assumption often made within the planning profession that 'open space often seemed to be imbued with almost magical powers to create a harmonious society'. However, she does acknowledge that open space may represent a different kind of zone within the city, one signalling a sense of freedom and escape.

The over–ordered city As more and more public space becomes commercialized and disciplined—shopping malls, muzak, CCTV, private security guards, car-dominated streets—the park acquires greater importance as a place where children can play with some degree of freedom, where people can develop varying degrees of private or personal relationships in public settings, where communities and interest groups can hold festivals or celebrations. In short, it becomes a realm of freedom. The park is still outside the ethos of consumption and can be contrasted with the way shopping centres control the flow of people through entrances, escalators and corridors. Margaret Crawford describes American malls as follows: 'Dramatic atriums create huge floating spaces for contemplation, multiple levels provide infinite vistas from a variety of vantage points and reflective surfaces bring near and far together...The resulting weightless realm receives substance only through the commodities it contains'.[23] The shopping centre is dragging the city inside (a fantasy of urbanism) and under cover, parks are still outside; flow through parks is free–form, the atmosphere—the micro–climate—is not controlled. The problem for public parks is to find ways of making them safe places without going down the consumerist road of creating an over–controlled environment devoid of any evidence of poverty, or indeed 'bad' weather. Such an approach would extinguish the sense of the park as a realm of freedom. 'Open space, like an open society must be free and yet controlled,' Lynch argued. Public parks need a paradigm of controlled freedom, but not one that mimics the consumerist model. Such a paradigm can be drawn from the positive aspects of urban life which are displayed in parks. Apart from large festivals, many smaller events and informal gatherings take place in hundreds of parks every summer weekend, including school sports days, half marathons, dog shows, fetes and religious events, as was noted earlier. Many of these events could only have happened in parks.

Flexible and reversible

Parks are adaptable and flexible places. For example, 40,000 people attended a Gay Pride event in Brockwell Park one weekend, and a couple of weekends later the park was used for the Lambeth Country Show, with tens of thousands attending that, too. For each event the park presented an apparently neutral backdrop against which the character and atmosphere of the event could be developed. When the events were over the park reverted to its former self with little or no trace of the festivals that had taken place. They avoid the 'white elephant' planning disaster syndrome of so much urban building, being 'multi–purpose' venues. And since the new watchwords of planning are flexibility and reversibility (if this scheme doesn't work, how much will it cost to dismantle it), then parks will continue to offer great opportunities for cultural renewal.

Limits to planning

Since the Victorian period and the emergence of the modern town planning profession, the role of public parks has been seen through planning terminology and processes, although the approach to parks and open space has undergone changes in recent decades.

> In the early part of the century, parks were seen as **islands** within the urban form, today open space is seen as the **setting** for cities.

The emphasis has been on 'greening the city' or drawing up 'green structure plans', in which green open space becomes the backdrop upon which the city is moulded. In a green structure plan, there is not only a green belt, but a green structure of open space networks, green-chain walks and nature conservation corridors, within which the city is embedded. These themes are current in the German approach to parks and planning and are described in Ralf Ebert's Working Paper 12 on Modern German Parks,[24] and Tom Turner's open space plan for London outlines a similar approach.[25] These green ideas link to the increasingly influential ecological standpoint but do not escape the limitations of the planning perspective. The rigid adherence to the demarcation of land as Metropolitan Open Space or as Green Belt has, in some instances, restricted the attempt to improve parks and open spaces, making them safer and more accessible. The scope for building in parks for example, and the opportunities for introducing new activities, people and events, are often excluded by current planning definitions. The far reaching implications of questions of safety, of sustainability, of urban regeneration, of new forms of management of open space will inevitably require a more flexible planning perspective.

THE PRESSURES FOR CHANGE   Section IV

This section looks at the way in which parks are reported and debated, and which pressure groups currently dominate thinking about parks policy.

Of the 8 million or so people who might statistically visit a park on any one day, the vast majority of them are unlikely to experience anything untoward. Yet parks are often only reported nationally when something terrible happens: for example, the murder of 9 year old Akhlaq Razzaq in Salt Hill Park, Slough in 1993, the murder of Rachel Nickell on Wimbledon Common, a boy of 14 bayoneted to death in an inter-school 'turf war' in Endcliffe Park, Sheffield in 1994. The park becomes associated in the public mind as a place of danger and arbitrary rape or attack, even though most kinds of violence, sexual attack and indeed murder happen within the home. Incidents in parks remain comparatively rare, and many local authorities keep incident books recording all untoward events or occurrences of criminal behaviour. *(margin: The park as an urban danger zone)*

This is not to minimise the fact that violent attacks, rapes and even murders do occasionally occur, but given the levels of usage of many parks, such incidents remain rare, so rare perhaps that they usually become national news. But the images of the park or recreation ground as dangerous territory are part of the stock images of TV crime series and soap operas (where location shooting is cheaper and less disruptive to do in parks), and so on. Often rumour becomes myth, and myth becomes local legend. Chiswick House Grounds in Hounslow had a legend of a girl drowning in a small pond, which when checked with police records proved to be false. *(margin: Popular (mis) representations)*

> 'Deterrents are more important than attractions in local people's decision as to whether to use their local park. On the other hand, incentives or inducements are more important for people coming from a distance. For local users, the choice essentially is: Park or No Park. For distant users, the choice is: That Park or Another Park (or Another Attraction).

(margin: Leicester Case Study Discussion Groups)

Parks are also perceived as dangerous for other reasons: as places where local social breakdown may be most displayed. The rise of urban homelessness has literally meant more people sleeping out rough, invariably in public places, and often—illicitly—in parks. Until a massive 'clean up' operation in 1994, up to 200 people were sleeping rough in Lincoln's Inn Fields, a public open space managed by Camden Council. York City Council applied to the Home Office in 1994 for permission to introduce a by–law making it an offence to drink alcohol in a number of 'designated places', which was wholly aimed at curbing groups of drinkers congregating in local parks, as have Bath, Belfast and Leamington Spa, among others.[26] Small pocket parks such as 'Itchy *(margin: Social breakdown)*

Park' in Spitalfields, Camberwell Green, and in dozens of other declining urban centres, have become places where 'the dispossessed' gather to meet, drink, and occasionally fight. However, again, the problem has to be seen in proportion.

Camberwell Green Case Study As part of the Southwark case study we observed the pattern of drinking at Camberwell Green—an increasingly typical city drinking place—over the summer, a source of much local discontent. In the end we realised that:

a)   there was more drinking going on outside the park than in it, whether in all day pubs, bus shelters, supermarket entrances, and so on; in fact the area itself was economically almost dependent on a drink culture;

b)   many of the drinkers were often very quiet, solitary, 'tidily dressed' people, with whom other park users often struck up a conversation—not 'a race apart';

c)   it was concluded that Camberwell Green, despite its problems, was still a major positive amenity in the area—a busy traffic–clogged, exhaust–polluted, siren–pierced, inner city road junction—a green haven and 'calming influence on the eyes and senses, in what is otherwise a frenetic and brittle street scene'.

In short, the park cannot compensate for society, but often acts to ameliorate the tensions. However there is a long way to go—and it is salutary to be reminded of some possible trends—before British parks reach the stage of some of those in North America, where, according to sociologist Mike Davis, McArthur Park, 'once the jewel in the crown of Los Angeles' park system, is now a free–fire zone where crack dealers and street gangs settle their scores with shotguns and Uzis. Thirty people were murdered there in 1990.' [27]

Who is arguing for change? The perceived 'crisis of parks' has resulted in a number of valuable interventions in the early 1990s, ranging from the continuing campaigning by the Open Spaces Society against any encroachment on urban open space, the Audit Commission report on *Competitive Management of Parks & Green Spaces* (HMSO 1988), the ILAM report, *A Strategic Approach to the Planning & Management of Parks & Open Spaces* (1991), *The Playing Pitch Strategy*, by the Sports Council, the NPFA & CCPR (1991), and the *LPAC Report on Open Space Planning in London* (Llewellyn Davis 1992), *City Gardens: An Open Spaces Survey in the City of London*, Corporation of London 1992, *Urban Parks: A Discussion Paper from the Landscape Institute* (1992), a report by The Garden History Society and The Victorian Society, *Public Prospects: Historic Urban Parks Under Threat* (1993), *Grounds for Concern: The GMB's campaign to defend our parks, gardens and open spaces* (1993), *Watch This Space!*, London Boroughs Association (1995), market research into the use of the Royal Parks (ongoing), together with many local surveys and campaigns. All this has provided valuable and graphic evidence attesting to the current parlous state of many of Britain's urban parks and open spaces.

Many of the given assumptions about parks and open spaces made in these reports might well be open to question, particularly in the light of the fiscal, social and cultural trends now massively impacting on modern urban life. Is it really true, as the Open Spaces Society continue to argue, that 'urban space is so vital, we need more.' There is ample evidence from this study, that too much open space, in the wrong places, can destroy the necessary densities and social mixes of urban life that make it socially sustainable.

Crying wolf

Similarly, is it really true, as the Sports Council, NPFA (National Playing Fields Association) & CCPR (Central Council for Physical Recreation) argued in 1991 in respect of an alleged loss of urban playing fields, that 'Public pitches also cater for informal sports, informal play, fairs and other occasional attractions, and a whole range of passive recreational uses such as sitting and picnicking. They have too an amenity and environmental value in providing physical, visual and aesthetic breaks in the urban form.' This assertion of the rich contribution made to urban living by playing fields and recreation grounds might well be doubted. The evidence from many of those now managing urban open space is that there are too many sports pitches and recreation grounds in some places, which are under–used, bleak and offer no ecological, aesthetic or social benefits other than to a very tiny section of the male population on a seasonal basis. As the Landscape Institute report says, 'It is estimated that in many parks only 6% of the users come for organised sports, but sport takes up 25% of the space and over 50% of the maintenance budget...There is a tendency for parks to promote male physical fitness, at the expense of children, women, family groups, the elderly and the disabled.' [28]

Too many pitches?

Yes

The NPFA, CCPR and Sports Council have also come together to produce the Registry of Recreation Land (May 1993), a database of sites and statistics of acquisition and loss of recreational spaces. One conclusion from the Register is that 'agreed and possible losses account for about 1.75% of existing sites.' It could be argued that this does not seem to be the major threat posed in the campaigning literature, and also lacks a strategic understanding as to whether this really is a problem at all. As Mike Collins argues in Working Paper 11, making up a shortfall of pitches where such a shortfall exists, might be better achieved by shifting demand from peak times, the transfer of some resources to artificial surfaces (plus evening floodlighting) for those who wish to play on them, and bringing more educational playing fields into use, rather than creating more under–used, green deserts. In short, thinking strategically about provision.

Playing Fields Count

Other patterns of recreation may mean that the traditional allocation of space to traditional male pitch sports is likely to change. Again Mike Collins identifies five major trends in patterns of physical recreation:

Patterns of recreation

(a) the development of **mini versions** of games to help children (mini rugby, unihoc, short tennis);

(b) the development of very strong **youth programmes** to counteract the demographic trends and the decline of sport in school; netball and hockey have been aided nationwide through grants and development officers as focus sports over the last three years by the Sports Council;

(c) the development of **indoor versions** of outdoor games—5–a–side football, cricket, bowls, tennis;

(d) the growth of **women's** participation;

(e) the growth of **new activities**.

Of particular note is the move of many outdoor sports into indoor arenas, where there is much greater flexibility for all day and evening use, irrespective of the weather or natural lighting conditions. It may be that the historic dominance of football over urban recreational space is weakening.

Heritage & conservation
Another powerful lobby for re–investment in urban parks is represented in the arguments put forward in Public Prospects by The Garden History Society and The Victorian Society. While their calls for more staffing to combat vandalism and encourage greater feelings of security are welcome, as is their concern for the pleasures of horticulture and 'passive' recreation, the continuing presumption against, for example, new buildings in parks seems ultimately counter–productive. The report cites the Midlands Arts Centre (MAC) development in Cannon Hill Park as showing 'little consideration for its park setting', whereas many might think it an ideal place to put an arts centre. Time and again the report cites 'historic character' as a reason for not developing anything new, such as a garden centre or a car park. Yet in Merton the development of a garden centre (with car park), cafe and arts studios in the National Trust owned, Morden Hall Park, encouraged by Merton Council, has re–invigorated that park. While admiring and endorsing many of the sentiments in favour of traditional Victorian park design, standards of horticulture and staffing levels, as well as the recommendation for individual park management plans, the lack of sympathy for modern social needs—there is no mention of children's play facilities of any kind, for example—diminishes the strength of the argument.

The ecology case
A more recent but increasingly powerful lobby arguing for more green space, and a re–thinking of traditional park forms—is that of the ecology lobby. The case for regarding parks as essentially urban ecological systems that might finally tame the city is that made by David Nicholson Lord in Working Paper No 4, *Calling in the Country: Ecology, Parks and Human Need*. Nicholson Lord's starting point is that 'modern cities are environmental disaster zones', and therefore the key role of parks is to ameliorate as best they can the polluting and degrading effects of urban living. He welcomes moves towards 'the greening of the city', with the

rise of city farms, ecological parks, nature gardens, greenway systems, community forests, and many other environmental initiatives, and calls for greater use to be made of urban open space for food production, wind farms, and other productive uses.

This is a powerful argument, and also has the merits of being based on genuine trends and initiatives in urban ecology. But, like the other arguments—including the one made in this report itself—it is of course partial. For it sometimes fails to address the inherently urban and social construction of parks—they are not always primarily 'natural' places. Whilst the principles of the ecology approach are extremely valuable, they cannot be applied to all urban open space. | Ecology and urbanity

It appears to us that in the early stages of the ecology movement, in reclaiming urban land, people's fears and mis–conceptions about what is now known as 'wildspace' were sometimes overlooked. The wild area in Inwood Park, Hounslow, for example, was often described by people we interviewed as 'the dog area', and was seen as an unregulated area that could attract undesirable characters. More recently urban ecology projects have been much more successful in creating links with local communities, particularly through education. Urban Wildlife Trusts have been at the forefront of generating interest and involvement in managing and maintaining ecological sites in cities. It is now clear that the population is now more ecology–minded than ever before.

The most active lobby for urban parks in recent years has been that of the landscape architecture profession. Their report, Urban Parks: A Discussion Paper from the Landscape Institute, seems much the best contribution to the debate in recent years, but again there has been a lack of attention to the detailed evidence of people's use of parks, their need perhaps for new kinds of spaces such as city farms, community gardens, specialised children's provision, and the report at times seems to revert to a partisan and vested interest case in more funding for new landscaping and design solutions, without raising the deeper questions of management and responsibility. There has also been a lack of understanding of just how difficult it is to manage and maintain good parks in hostile and impoverished inner city environments, as if it were all simply a matter of good design. Professional groups such as landscape architects, architects or artists should be seen as contributors to a team effort which also involves the skills and knowledge of park users. | Design solutions

Landscape architects are increasingly influential in park debates, and in a social and political vacuum, they can come to dominate. This is not just a problem in Britain. Herbert Muschamp, the architecture critic of the New York Times, has recently written about an exhibition in New York called New Park: New Ideas, which he found seriously wanting. | Ethics or aesthetics?

'What we saw was a series of landscape designs presented as though they were landscape paintings. What we saw, in other words, was a classic example of the hegemony of visual culture—of the dominance of visual images over other kinds of content. If there is one place where that hegemony should be challenged, it is in the design of new parks. We need to know not only how parks look but also how they work.'[29]

This is part of the wider problem of urban regeneration schemes, particularly around public space, where in David Harvey's words, aesthetics has triumphed over ethics.

Missing Persons Not surprisingly, the trade union to which many parks workers belong, the GMB, has undertaken its own campaign called 'Grounds for Concern'. Not only have there been serious losses of jobs in local authority parks in recent years, but further cuts are still on the agenda in 4 out of 5 local authorities, it is claimed. 'One in three councils said they anticipated job losses,' the GMB conclude, although no actual figures or estimates of figures are currently given. Staff training has been reduced or even cut completely in many local authorities.

> Campaigners for improving Finsbury Park in North London claim that when the park was handed over to the Haringey Council by the GLC in 1986 there were 10 keepers and 13 gardeners as well as 13 other park–based staff. In 1994 they claimed there were no longer any dedicated full–time keepers. [30]

Certainly the public perceive this loss of staffing, and it is perhaps the most common cause of complaint about park decline, even if mobile maintenance crews (whether direct labour or contracted) still maintain existing standards of upkeep. The GMB also point out that traditionally 'local councils have often used horticulture departments as a way of fulfilling wider community objectives,' citing the examples of the many disabled ex-serviceman who were given work after the war in nurseries and parks, as well as providing sheltered employment for those with learning disabilities. They have won the support of MEN-CAP in their campaign to ensure that contracting out doesn't mean an end to these important social objectives.

The political agenda Lastly, but in the end perhaps most importantly, one should ask where the future of parks lies on the local government political agenda? In Sheffield, for example, local people dis-satisfied with the political response to the decline of Sheffield's parks have even stood 'Save Our Parks and Services' candidates in the 1994 local elections, winning respectable support though not any seats. For some local politicians the more difficult choices of developing strategies, looking seriously at management issues, and in the end making difficult and locally contentious decisions about prioritising some places rather than others, or of sharing power and responsibility with community organisations, or even devolving power completely, are still being avoided.

Despite the constraints on local government spending imposed by central government, even if they were to be relaxed, the decline of urban parks cannot be reversed by money alone. The arguments for parks have yet to be made in the language that modern politics demands. It is not surprising that, amongst the competing claims of social services, housing, anti–poverty strategies, crime and safety issues, and without clear evidence and arguments, parks are regarded as still being of marginal concern.

Furthermore, the difficult question as to whether local authorities can continue as the sole managing agency and provider of so many different public services has been raised by members and officers alike in many places. But we would want to ask, given that local government still retains the crucial elements of democratic accountability and local distinctiveness, if it cannot currently cope, how can it be supported, encouraged, and helped to do so?

Section V PARK LIFE TODAY: THE RESEARCH FINDINGS

The following section reports on the findings of the observation exercises, the interviews, the household surveys and group discussions carried out as part of the case-study work. The observation exercises were carried out in eight different parks and the interviews were held in ten parks. The household surveys were carried out in Southwark and in Cardiff. The findings are summarised in this section, and a fuller version is to be found in Appendix 1. Discussion groups were held in Bristol, Bromley, Dublin, Hounslow, Leicester, Middlesbrough, Merton and Greenwich. Overall, 10,250 people were observed, 1,211 people interviewed and 295 household questionnaires were returned.

THE OBSERVATION EXERCISE

For the purposes of the study, an observation exercise and survey form was devised to administer in parks, briefly noting down the characteristics of all people entering a particular park on a particular day. Observers were positioned to cover all entrances and exits. The form was designed to note park users according to:

- gender

- entering the park with or without a baby in a pushchair (hence age and sex indeterminate)

- entering a park with a dog or dogs

- approximate age group,

- alone or with others

- ethnicity (White/Afro–Caribbean/Asian)

- physical disability.

In all, 10,250 people were observed during the summer of 1994, mostly on Sundays, and in eight different parks, some of which were surveyed on more than one occasion. The parks were: Poulter Park (LB Sutton), Albert Park (Middlesbrough), Inwood Park (LB Hounslow), Maryon Park (LB Greenwich), Victoria Park (Cardiff), Brunswick Gardens (LB Southwark), St Andrew's Park (Bristol) and Charlton Park (LB Greenwich). In all cases the park observation exercise was a constituent feature of the local case study. It was also often the first occasion for a long time when actual numbers of users had been counted. Lampton Park and Heston Park in Hounslow, and Abbey Park in Leicester were also observed, and counts taken, albeit with slightly different questionnaires and methodology. A brief profile of the parks follows.

PARKS OBSERVED

St Andrews: a small park at the centre of a residential suburb of Bristol   BRISTOL
characterised by owner occupied Victorian housing with gardens.

Victoria Park: a 20 acre park to the west of Cardiff City centre. In many   CARDIFF
ways it is a typical Victorian park with ornamental flower beds and
mature trees.

Charlton Park: a 42 acre park with a Jacobean Manor House at one end   GREENWICH
and an extensive area of playing fields and football pitches at the other.
Maryon Park: a medium sized ornamental park in an area of Greenwich
characterised by local authority rented property, purpose built flats and
relatively low levels of car ownership.

Inwood Park: a medium sized park set in a residential area of semi–de-   HOUNSLOW
tached housing about 1/4 of a mile from Hounslow town centre.
Lampton Park: a large park adjoining the borough's Civic Centre on
one side and allotments on the other, containing tennis courts, extensive playing fields and some formal planting. **Heston Park**: a small
local park to the north of the borough, surrounded by housing and
abutting the leisure centre and library.

Abbey Park: Leicester's major city park contains a great range of fea-   LEICESTER
tures—a small zoo, model railway, boating lake, historic ruins, playing
fields and formal flower beds. It is crossed by the River Soar and runs
alongside the canal.

Albert Park: town park, residential hinterland, accessible by public   MIDDLESBROUGH
transport, attractive landscaping, boating lake, putting green, bowling
pavilion and green, ornamental flower–beds, tree–lined walks, a focus
for early evening jogging, student football and impromptu team
games, significant ethnic minority use, modern children's playground.

Poulter Park: a 50 acre park with a large area of playing fields and an   SUTTON
under–used 19th century country house. The residential area around
the park is characterised by low rise semi–detached local authority
housing.

Brunswick Park: a small park in a very mixed residential area charac-   SOUTHWARK
terised by owner–occupied Victorian housing and housing divided into
flats and occupied by less affluent home sharers.

This 'broad brush' survey, the first of its kind as far as we know in the
UK, should be treated with some caution obviously. It took place during one of the hottest summers on record, and almost always on Sunday. Seasonal and weekday variations are likely to be significant. Yet its
findings are complemented by the questionnaire administered, which
sought to monitor and record more general patterns of use. The main
findings were that:

Gender   Of the 10,250 park users observed, 6,114 were male and 4,136 female, giving an average ratio across all age groups of male users to women users of 60%:40%. In general the 6:4 ratio was reflected almost uniformly across all parks.

Babies & buggies   A separate record was kept of very young babies either carried into the park or pushed in a pram or buggy. This was a fairly infrequent occurrence, making up as little as 1% of the total count, and never more than 5%.

Dogs   The presence of dogs in parks remains one of the most contentious issues in current park management and public concern. Again this survey may be one of the first to quantify the issue. Averaged out across all the parks surveyed, the ratio of dogs to humans was 1:8.

Age groups   Two age categories—Young Adults and Middle Aged—made up more than 50% of all park users. There may be two areas of surprise or concern which would warrant further investigation—the significant use made of parks by teenagers and young adults (often perceived as 'anti–social' age groups), and the significant under–representation of the elderly.

Alone or with others   Approximately one third of people observed entering parks came on their own, one third came with one other person, and a final third of park users came as part of a larger group. Even the people who came alone were often those accompanied by a dog or dogs. Women on their own were a sight sufficiently unusual to warrant particular comment by observers on the observation sheets.

Ethnicity   Ethnicity is also connected with group use. In general it was found that ethnic minority use of parks quite closely followed local demographic patterns of ethnic minority representation in the local population. However ethnic minority use is more patterned and time–governed. Asian use is family–based or group–based, and occurs mostly during the early evening and at weekends, particularly on Sunday afternoons. Afro–Caribbean family use appears to follow the same pattern.

Disabled people   The observation exercise was designed to record the presence of people with evident physical disabilities, but such users never amounted to more than 0.5% of all users, and again this is an area of park use that requires further investigation, given that disabled people form 10% of the population.

INTERVIEWS WITH PARK USERS

In conjunction with the observation exercise, short interviews were carried out with park users. The questionnaire was designed to elicit basic information about the way people used the parks. In all, 1,211 people were interviewed on 10 separate dates in 10 different parks.

Very broadly this figure represents more than 10% (11.8%) of the number of people observed using the parks. The main findings were:

The results from all the surveys show that the majority of park users interviewed live close to the parks they use. 68% of users said it took them less than five minutes to get to the park.

Travel time

People walk to parks. Strikingly, the figures from all the surveys show that more than 69% of all those interviewed in every park walked to the park.

Means of travel

Park users tend to visit their local park very frequently. In every survey but one, more than 40% of people interviewed said they visited the park daily. (It should be noted that dog–walking accounts for a lot of people using parks on a daily basis.)

Frequency of use

The majority of people interviewed in all the parks thought they would spend up to 30 minutes in the park. Clearly, time spent in the park is dependent upon variable factors such as the weather conditions. Nevertheless, there does appear to be a discernible pattern which suggests that the majority of visitors stay for short periods but significant minorities (20– 30%) stay for an hour or more in the parks.

Time spent in the park

Perhaps unsurprisingly (since these people were already in the parks) people interviewed did not generally feel unsafe in the park during the day. In most instances more than 70% of people said that they had not been deterred from using the park.

Feelings about safety

Defining why people visit parks is notoriously difficult. People may have many reasons, some may be to do with the attractions of the park, others may be more to do with getting out, getting away or finding a place to talk. Nevertheless, taking children to parks does seem to be an important factor behind many park visits. Taking dogs for walks is also a clear reason for park use.

Reasons for visiting the park

The majority of people in all the surveys said they visited the country-side outside their towns or cities once a month or a few times a year. The numbers of people who said they never visited the countryside were significant, particularly those people living in London. 43% of those interviewed in Southwark said they never visited. In Greenwich the figures were 34% & 39% on two different occasions.

Visiting the countryside

Most surveys show that the majority of people had access to a private garden. More than 78% of all those interviewed had their own or shared a private garden.

Access to a garden

The survey results suggest that car ownership is generally lower than garden ownership. An average of 54% of people across all the surveys had access to a car. The surveys in Sutton, Hounslow and Cardiff showed the highest levels of car ownership. Again the figures for Maryon Park in Greenwich and Brunswick park in Southwark show the

Access to a car

lowest levels of car ownership. 70% of those interviewed in Southwark and 56% of people interviewed in Maryon Park did not have access to a car.

HOUSEHOLD SURVEYS IN CARDIFF & SOUTHWARK

Another element of the quantitative research involved two household surveys, conducted in Cardiff and Southwark. Victoria Park, Cardiff is a 20 acre 'town park' in a mixed residential area of Cardiff, well maintained, and with tennis courts, bowling green, paddling pool, children's play area, toilet block and other traditional park amenities. Sunray Gardens is a small, ornamental gardens, again in a mixed residential area, in which the main—and very attractive—feature is an ornamental pond with weeping willows, as well as tennis courts and children's play area.

Completion Rate
The majority of the questionnaires were completed by women (Cardiff 63%, Southwark 61%), and the majority of responses came from the 25–45 age group. In both places approximately 20% of questionnaires distributed were returned, representing nearly 50% of households returning at least one, a high response rate which suggests something of the value and interest that local people place on parks issues.

Frequency of Use
34% of Cardiff people and 35% of Southwark respondents stated that they had visited the park that day, and an additional 32% of Cardiff people and 41% of Southwark respondents said that they had visited the named park within the past 7 days.

The main reasons people gave for visiting were:

REASONS FOR USE

	Cardiff	Southwark
To go for a walk	32%	29%
To accompany a child	21%	27%
Taking a short cut	17%	15%
To play	12.5%	14%

Only 10% of Cardiff respondents and 5% of Southwark respondents gave exercising a dog as a reason, though this is clearly a major reason which many people will not admit to.

Likes and Dislikes
Because the two parks are very different, what people most liked about each park varied, namely in Cardiff the most popular element of the park were the 'Flowers/Trees' (27%) but in Southwark it was the 'Pond' (23%). Play areas also scored high in people's responses to a choice of favourite features. The things people disliked were much more diverse, although one factor—dog excrement—was mentioned by 38% of Cardiff and 27% of Southwark respondents, by far the highest single cause of concern.

Questions of safety produced some very interesting results. The majority of respondents (92% Cardiff and 86% Southwark) claimed to feel
safe in the park in daylight hours, with only 4% Cardiff and 9%
Southwark claiming not to feel safe (and 5% in both surveys making
no comment). Yet as a percentage, slightly more males than females
claimed to feel unsafe in the park during daylight hours in both samples. Safety is often self–limiting and self–imposed. Feeling safe when
you visit the park on a sunny morning is not the same as feeling safe at
all times.

Questions of safety

OPEN ENDED QUESTIONS

The questionnaire conducted with park users in the parks included two
open ended questions asking people about possible improvements and
any other comments about the park. The interviewers recorded the answers and additional comments people made. The following is a summary of the comments made. They reflect some of the views of current
park users.

Introduction

The ideas and concerns people expressed followed similar themes, despite the range of parks within which the surveys were conducted and
the distinctive features of each one. The three themes most frequently
referred to were the need to control dogs and remove dog excrement,
requests for the re-introduction of parks keepers and the need to improve park maintenance.

Dogs, keepers, maintenance

Comments about the need for park keepers were often a kind of short
hand for the much wider question of dealing with and preventing
anti–social behaviour, vandalism and other criminal activity. The park
keeper is a symbol of order, care and control. Many people considered
that the problems of their parks would be greatly reduced by the presence of a park keeper. The lack of a park keeper seemed to suggest that
the park was somehow incomplete. The presence of staff in the park is
seen as a key to unlocking the full potential of the park, as one woman
said *'I've known the park all my life—there is a lack of respect for it compared to years
ago… A perimeter fence would help to keep motorbikes out. There should be well–defined
car parks. The presence of attendants would keep down vandals. This park has so much
potential…'*

Symbolic role

'Get the yobs out!' Vandalism was clearly of great concern to many park
users, but this concern is not simply directed towards young people. It
reflects a wider mistrust and discomfort with the behaviour of 'other'
people generally—anti–social behaviour such as undisciplined children, the practice of allowing dogs to run loose, the use of motorbikes
in parks, and activity seen as dangerous such as golf practice and even
cycling.

Yob culture

More facilities Many people remarked on the need for more facilities such as cafes, kiosks, toilets, shelters, telephones, benches, litter bins, lighting, signs, better tennis courts, open air pools, paddling pools and better children's playgrounds. These features are all facilities that might reasonably be found in a park. In fact pleas were frequently made for the restoration of facilities that may have once existed, such as drinking fountains, lidos, putting greens and flowers. 'There's too much vandalism and it needs some flowers'. Many concerns were minor but important to users, parents mentioned the need for seats and picnic tables in play areas, an elderly user asked for 'Proper seating, not those low things you can't get out of.'

Close to home The proximity of the park to home was in part a matter of convenience for many people, however, it also reflected an attachment and affection towards the park as a distinct feature of the locality. Many people commented on the fact that they liked the park because it was close to home and part of their local area.

Don't change it 'It's perfect as it is.' Many people wished to record their appreciation of the park and genuinely didn't think it could be improved upon. As one person commented, when asked to suggest possible improvements: 'Fine weather and good company' was all that was needed. Many of the comments made in Victoria Park in Cardiff referred to the 'lovely flower beds'.

DISCUSSION GROUPS

Introduction As part of the research for individual case–studies several groups of people were brought together to discuss their views and attitudes towards particular parks. Sessions were held with teenagers, young mothers, with students, with elderly people, with disabled people, with residents groups and with Asian women. These groups were not intended to be representative of the population at large; they were selected in order to explore particular issues connected with the subject of the case–studies. Nevertheless, from these discussions we have drawn out themes that reflect the preoccupations and attitudes towards public parks of those who took part.

PARKS AND CHILDREN

People associate parks with children and childhood. The perception that parks are places for children and that children are the most legitimate users of public parks was commonly expressed. Even people who were regular park users themselves saw the primary justification of public parks as places for children. Many talked of their own memories of playing in parks as children. Often these memories contrasted with people's current perceptions of parks as run down and neglected.

Concerns about the current poor state of parks were often expressed in terms of how they affect children. Anxiety about vandalism, broken glass, dogs, the presence of alcoholics were expressed as threats to children's use of parks. In one public meeting people stood up and articulated and justified their anger about the current state of their local parks in terms of the effect on children's use. They described the parks they had loved as children that had become no go places for their own children or grandchildren. In contrast, good parks were thought to offer children freedom and in particular, freedom from traffic, widely felt to be a constant constraint on their behaviour. Questions of personal safety were also often expressed as worries for the safety of children. The comment that '*It's OK for me but I wouldn't like my children to go alone*' was frequently made.

Many park users regard themselves as 'surrogate' users: their main reason for using the park is to bring their children or grandchildren. These adults did not consider that they were using the park for themselves, but that they were there only to accompany children. '*Taking the children*' is frequently used as a general explanation for family trips to the park, but, as one woman in Bristol said, going to the park '*is a good chance to meet up as a large family, especially when our sitting room is so small*'.

Taking the children

Park visits provided a way for children to spend time with one or other parent after a separation or divorce. '*We used to meet our dad in the park when he left home*'. Taking children to the parks was also described by people as an opportunity for parents to talk to children; '*I think its the only chance a lot of people have to show children the variety of life, everything from trees and plants to animals*'.

Weekend visits

Parents in discussion groups expressed great concern about the danger of loose dogs and dog excrement. The threat of contracting toxicara from dog excrement has become yet another facet of child safety for which parents have to take responsibility and precautions. For some, picnics at the park have become simply too unpleasant and a potential health risk. Children and dogs don't mix. The need to control dogs is seen by many parents as a prerequisite to any qualitative change to urban open space. Disabled groups in Leicester talked about the problem that dog excrement caused for the visually impaired.

Loose dogs

The most obvious attraction for children in parks is the children's playground. They are standard and symbolic features of public parks. Yet it is not always the presence of a playground that attracts use by children and their parents. Women in Merton and Bromley talked of the greater appeal water and animals had for their children. Mothers in one group said they did not visit the playground in their nearest park but preferred to walk or drive further to a town centre park which had a duck pond, as the ducks and water interested their young children much more. In Merton, the mothers' group described the way in which the presence of a paddling pool turned a run down neighbourhood park into a crowded local facility. '*On a hot day you have to get there early to claim a place by the pool*'. Abbey Park interviewees in Leicester put water features at the top of their list of preferred places. Water was appreciated both actively (ducks, boating, model boats), and passively (many people were observed just standing watching the water). City Farms also

Water and animals

WILDLIFE

appeal strongly to children; the survey in Heeley City Farm Sheffield showed that '*to bring children*' was by far the main reason people gave for their visit.

A meeting point Well–used children's playgrounds can become a local meeting point for parents and children. A good example of this was given by a woman in Bristol who told the story of how she had a 'log reunion' in the park. When her children were young, she and other mothers would meet by a log in the play area. The women, some of whom are now grandmothers, recently held a reunion. They decided that the best and most apt place for their reunion was the log in the park.

Discussions with children In two of the case–studies, discussions were held with children in schools to find out more about their attitudes and use of the local parks. In one group of very young children the words 'park' and 'playground' were used interchangeably. For them a park is a playground. Although the playgrounds they imagined, drew and described were a far cry from the standard set piece facilities offered in most parks. Places for imaginary games, such as tree houses and play houses, figured strongly in their drawings and the children explained them as places to hide, to talk and play. Riding bikes was also important. A high number of the children in Merton and Bromley said they had bikes and the park was one of the few places where they could ride them.

Safety The children were highly aware of adult concerns for their safety and talked of having to stay indoors unless they were accompanied by an older child or an adult, but their immediate fears were related to vandalism (broken glass in the play areas) and bullying. The older children of 10 and 11 were more likely to be allowed to use the parks without adults but usually had to be accompanied by friends. In Leicester, Asian schoolboys talked about the threat of racism and of physical harassment in general. Questions of safety were not the only negative features identified. In Bromley the children listed dog excrement, lack of bins and seating, inadequacy of playground equipment, dangerous equipment, lack of lighting, fear of adolescents, locked toilets and the sense that there is no-one to go to if there was trouble, as the main problems of the park. They were also critical of the bland landscape in many parks—'*it all looks the same*'—and of the lack of facilities for the disabled or for the elderly.

The children involved were full of ideas about how parks could be improved. Their suggestions tended to apply to the whole park and not simply to the cordoned off children's playground. As well as more adventurous equipment for abseiling, rope walks, soft landings, assault courses, and bike tracks, they suggested quiet areas, a maze, garden ponds, and places to worship. As well as simply listing facilities, they described ways they could get involved through events in the park, music bands, festivals, in managing wildlife areas and having the opportunity to garden in their own allotments.

Despite the overwhelming association people make between parks and children—'*the park is a godsend for children*'—the actual expenditure on children is relatively limited and the design and planning for children is mostly restricted to small playgrounds. As Bob Hughes points out in his paper, a very small percentage of total leisure expenditure is spent on children. [31] In public parks, the money that is spent on children is likely to be for children's playgrounds. Children's playgrounds are a standard feature of many parks. Action for Play in Sheffield is a collection of parents groups raising money for play equipment, which is often matched by Council funding.

Expenditure on children

> 'A recent report from the National Playing Fields Association estimates that the Department of Heritage spends 3p on the needs of children for every £100 spent on adult leisure.'

Source:
Independent on Sunday 23/1/94

A good children's playground provides an attraction, its presence welcomes children to the park and provides a meeting point for parents. However, a large number of children's playgrounds are of poor quality, with minimal and limited play equipment, and this, according to one experienced leisure manager we spoke to, may simply reflect the dominant position of men in parks management. In many instances the money spent on the provision and routine repair of poor quality children's playgrounds could be better spent on children in other ways. It is often assumed that children don't particularly notice if the playground is a bit rundown or desultory, but, as Wendy Titman's research on the way children understand their environment shows, children are very adept at picking up messages about the landscapes and environments adults care for. They are well aware of the poor quality of much of the environment around their homes and schools.[32]

Best use of resources?

> Coram's Fields is a specialist children's playground near Great Ormond Street Hospital. The playground is run as a children's only facility. Adults are not allowed into the playground unless accompanied by a child. It is owned by a trust. It is not a public park and the trust is therefore able to stipulate this rule. The playground is run by 3 staff members and additional staff run the pets corner, a crèche and after school care. During the summer school holidays Coram's Field has up to 1,500 children a day in the park.

CORAM'S FIELDS,
LONDON

> The large play area (1 hectare) was refurbished in 1990. It is part of a much larger public Victorian park. The play area now has a reputation as one of the best children's playgrounds in the country. There is enough play equipment to keep children from 0 – 18 happy. It is free and always busy. At weekends the playground draws families from up to 30 or 40 miles away. The playground has picnic tables, toilets, changing facilities and play attendants. Dogs are banned from the play area. In many ways the play equipment is conventional—swings, roundabouts, slides, climbing frames and skateboard ramps. However, the area works because of a 'critical mass' of equipment, it ensures that the area is busy and more likely to be safe.

VICTORIA PARK,
BATH

TEENAGE USE

One of the most significant findings of the research (Bromley, Greenwich, Middlesbrough, Leicester, Bristol) is how important parks are to young people, whether parks managers or other users like them or not. All the discussions with teenagers showed they had extensive knowledge of the parks in their area.

A place to hang out
Our discussions with young people began to show the extent to which teenagers use public parks as places to hang out. They knew them from childhood. A group of girls in Bristol, described the way they spent much of their free time in parks, particularly during the summer. 'If all the parks were bashed down now, I don't know what half the people would do—there'd be nothing to do'. For them the parks were seen as a relatively safe environment—'If you walk round the streets you get called names, like slag, whore. In the parks I find it a lot safer than I do outside on the streets. More people get grabbed out on the street than in parks'. That's not to say they were not critical, they were highly critical of poor maintenance and were sometimes concerned about the presence of other young people in the park. 'The older kids haven't got anywhere else to go. They sit there and smoke and drink and throw bottles everywhere and set things on fire, smashing the park up. They write things, break the trees'. These teenage girls were often responsible for taking younger children, brothers and sisters and neighbours' children, to the park and so were aware of the dangers of broken glass and defective play equipment. Asian young people in Hounslow talked about pressure at home, leading them to use the park as their major meeting point.

Private places
One park in Bromley is used every evening by local teenagers as a place to meet and talk. It has been used in this way by a changing group of teenagers for the last 10 years. The group meet almost every night of the week and stay in the park until 10pm or later. They are among the most frequent and constant of park users. They were aware that their presence in the park is sometimes seen as threatening to others, but for the most part the park is deserted after dark and few people realised they were there. During the day the 'rec' is open to everybody, at night it becomes 'their' park.

Exclusion
The park is a place of last resort, a place for young people to go when they've run out of money: 'I'd rather go to the cinema or the town centre' or when they've been moved out of the town centre. 'We used to go to the Galleries, but you're not allowed any more. You get shoved out by their security guards'. For this reason the young people taking part in these groups were less enthusiastic about the idea of re-introducing park keepers.

Child or adult
The girls in one group still enjoyed using the play equipment, although this caused resentment and hostility from parents with smaller children. The young women expressed a strong sense of injustice when asked by other adults to leave the children's play area: 'No, it's not your park'. There is conflict between adults and teenagers over what is considered acceptable behaviour, as a teenage boy in Greenwich ex-

plained: 'I like using the swings, but they won't let me, they say I'm too big—we sit on the swings to stop getting wet—if the grass is wet we sit on the swings'.

A second group in Bristol described another park as a social centre: 'It's the place where everyone goes'; 'It makes you feel closer to everyone else, even though they might live quite a long way off'. It's a place to meet people and stay there for the evening. Although it's not always benign; young people described fights and clashes between individuals and groups. One described the park as a place to 'grow up in—you go through every stage in the park'.

Social centre

Young people describe parks as places to flirt and places to meet boyfriends and girlfriends. Young people perceive that there is a great deal of hypocrisy about adult disapproval of their use of the park, particularly at night. As one young Bristol teenager said, 'there's flirting and stuff, closeness, kissing perhaps, but nobody gets on top of each other'. An older resident, talking about the same park, at least did admit that, 'When I was a teenager the park had fairly thick bushes all around the edges and the behaviour in the bushes was far worse than the behaviour you see outside the bushes nowadays. Despite the park keeper. Certainly there was sexual behaviour behind those bushes'. Parks have always been used for early sexual explorations and encounters—it may be one of their functions.

Discovering sex

Teenagers in Greenwich and Bristol described the parks as a place to go to when upset or angry. 'For me parks are a nice place to go if you're angry'. They described 'kicking the tree and the rosebuds' or 'booting a football, imagine it's someone's head you don't like', as harmless ways of releasing anger and avoiding hurting family or friends. They also described going to parks as an escape from family pressures. In Middlesbrough, Greenwich and Bristol, similar comments were made about getting away—'you can get away from your mum nagging', 'sometimes I escape from doing housework and run out to the park', or 'the parks are just somewhere to go—you can get away from the family and your annoying little brother'.

An escape

Over the last 15 years a new tradition of music events in parks has been established. Some are large festivals, the radio roadshows, and large-scale concerts such as Take That in Crystal Palace Park; others are smaller showcases for local bands. These events are perhaps the most successful form of provision for young people in parks.

Programming for young people

> One of Britain's main Irish music festivals for young people is the Finsbury Park Fleadh, which attracts tens of thousands of young people on one weekend a year—much to the disgruntlement of some local residents.

Some festivals attract opposition from local residents. However, if they are part of an organised programme of a limited number of events, particularly to benefit young people who have few other resources, then it does not seem such an unreasonable proposition. Although, as one Council officer has said, 'brave' councils could do much more in the way of festivals and music events in parks, if they were prepared to confront and manage the problems that go with them.

Some park authorities are beginning to take a more systematic approach to festivals. The Parks Trust in Milton Keynes has adapted an area of Campbell Park into a terraced, roman–style, grassed amphitheatre. Electricity, water and sewage services were incorporated into the design and the ranger staff can put up a set of marquees and stages in a matter of hours. The arena, an inconspicuous area of the park when not in use, can be quickly adapted to host music and theatre events.

A question of management

There is no doubt that teenage use of parks causes concern among adult park users. The comments made in the survey of Victoria Park Cardiff, showed that 'yobbish' behaviour was third, after dog excrement and poor maintenance, in people's lists of the worst aspects of the park. As young people themselves admit, their activities do sometimes cause damage. The common reaction amongst parks managers is to regard teenagers with suspicion and see them as a nuisance. Young people are often not seen as legitimate users of the park. Young people's use of the park could be managed more effectively so that it does not spoil enjoyment for other users. For example, if they tend to congregate around the children's play areas at night leaving beer cans and graffiti, then cleaning schedules might be altered and the parks cleaned first thing in the morning so that rubbish is removed and the swings are unravelled before parents and young children arrive.

OLDER PEOPLE

The observation exercises showed that elderly people were under–represented as park users both in comparison with other age groups and in proportion to their presence in the residential areas surrounding the parks. The research carried out by the London Borough of Bromley showed that the elderly were worried by the behaviour of the young, and that they saw the problems of society at large arising from the fact that young people did not have enough to do. The research also showed that taking grandchildren was an important reason for park visits.[33]

Balance between users

The discussion groups with elderly people in Bristol and Middlesbrough, also identified the behaviour of the young as one of the factors that put them off parks visits. For these people the parks had become dominated by one group and the sense that the park catered for different groups and different uses had been lost. In the past the park keeper used to mediate between different and conflicting groups of users. '*The presence of the park keeper meant that the lads would behave better and the standard of care of equipment and planted areas much higher*'. The groups felt that different users have different needs. For example, footballers, people with young children and the elderly each need to be able to use the parks. The fears older people expressed were not necessarily fears about being attacked but of being accidentally knocked over, hit by a football or having their glasses broken. '*I don't mind them playing football but it should be fenced off. I could have my glasses broken quite easily*'. The groups defended the right of young people to use the parks and the importance of the park as a place to meet friends, but for them what was important was the sense of balance between different groups of users and this is what had been lost over recent years. They felt that a park keeper would represent their interests and the balance between users would be restored.

The Bristol group saw their park as a place to socialise: '*usually you work in the garden, and you're on your own, but if you go to the park you usually see someone you know*'. It is a focal point of the residential area. Other green spaces in the city such as the newly pedestrianised area by the Cathedral were seen '*not as a place you go to, but you go through*' and although they might sit down for a while, these spaces did not have the same meaning for them as their own park.

A place to go to

The group in Middlesbrough also expressed the value of the parks as a place for social activity. '*It's very relaxing to walk through the park, even in the winter there's something to see*'.

Always something to see

Taking grandchildren to the park provided one of the main reasons for park visits, but once they've grown up the justification for going falls away. '*It's not safe on your own and I've no children to take now. I only used to go for the kids, I've enough to do in the garden and my kids like to go to the country now*'.

A PRIVATE PLACE IN A PUBLIC WORLD?

What came across most strongly in the discussion groups and in the comments made to interviewers undertaking the individual question-naires, was the sense that the park was a place where people con-sciously or unconsciously marked the passage of their lives: their memories of childhood games and 'playing out'; their wilder teenage years and early courting phase; a place for wedding photographs, and later taking their own children to the park to play and for picnics; later still taking grandchildren, and then finally, in some cases, marking the loss of a loved one by the commissioning of a memorial bench. It wasn't always the same park of course, though a number of people reminded the interviewers that they had '*been coming to this park for more than seventy years*'. The strength of feeling which many people exhibited in talking about 'their' park confirmed the uniqueness of such places within the wider pattern of urban life. For while everything else in the city changes, or so it seems, the park stays the same, and becomes a repository for popular memory, and therefore a key symbolic feature in the local sense of place.

Rites of passage

In this sense, then, it fulfils many of the functions of the sacred grove—a focus for the more spiritual aspects of people's lives in a secular society. For some, as was observed, it is a confessional, where people meet to sit on benches for hours on end, confiding, gossiping, laughing, or unravelling their cares and burdens. It is a place where

The sacred grove

people conduct relationships and often end them. In Middlesbrough one of the marriage guidance agencies recommends that estranged couples meet in Albert Park to discuss joint worries, and sometimes even the prospects of reconciliation, since a park is both a very public place and a very private place at the same time. Its openness lessens the tensions of a formal meeting room, and allows people to get up and go as they wish, and lessens the chances of anger and even violence because of its public nature. People go to parks to read, to write post-cards, letters and poems—to be private in a public place. All this was evident in almost every park observed.

Subverting the rules   In many ways the idea of a natural landscape in the middle of a town or city is an anomaly. Nature was imported by the Victorians into the city, as a form of escape or as a place where the pressures of the city could be avoided for a while, but also the city expanded to incorporate rural estates. In this process the park has come to mean—and maybe always has meant—a place where other rules and forms of behaviour are tolerated. Certainly this was true of the Victorian pleasure garden which came into its own at night and was the place where all kinds of sexual liaisons were negotiated under cover of darkness.

This ambivalence is precisely caught in Robert Pogue Harrison's great historical work on the symbolic meaning of the forest in Western culture, a meaning which urban parks often embody in some residual form:

> 'If forests appear in our religions as places of profanity, they also appear as sacred. If they have typically been considered places of lawlessness, they have also provided havens for those who took up the cause of justice and fought the law's corruptions. If they evoke associations of danger and abandon in our minds, they also evoke scenes of enchantment. In other words, in the religions, mythologies and literatures of the West, the forest appears as a place where the logic of distinction goes astray. Or where our subjective categories are confounded. Or where perceptions become promiscuous with one another, disclosing latent dimensions of time and consciousness. In the forest the inanimate may suddenly become animate, the god turns into a beast, the outlaw stands for justice, Rosalind appears as a boy, the virtuous knight degenerates into a wild man, the straight line forms a circle, the ordinary gives way to the fabulous.'

In many places throughout the world, the urban park plays this role as a stage set or background to sexual meetings, negotiations and fulfilments. As a number of people said in discussion, sexual encounters have always been a part of local park life. And while generally this is tolerated or ignored, homosexual encounters and liaisons continue to evoke particular fears and apprehensions. This has often taken the form of campaigns to close park toilets because they have been used as meeting places for homosexuals, or police trawls of well known gay meeting places such as Hampstead Heath or Highbury Fields in London. A recent film, 'Young Soul Rebels', by the young Black film–maker Isaac Julian, was largely based around the Black gay night–time scene in a Hackney park, which takes place largely without any awareness of it by many people living near or adjacent to the park.

These issues have been raised in a number of the case studies, and in fact we received a written submission about the Leicester case study from the Leicestershire based Men's Sexual Health Project. They have pointed out that many of the popular stereotypes of homosexual activity (often engaged in by men who regard themselves as heterosexual) are based in mythology. Fears of paedophilia (a common focus for concern about allowing children to use park toilets) is not supported by research which shows that 97% of child sexual abuse is perpetrated by heterosexual men, and mostly in the home. They have also pointed to a current police–supported scheme in Leicestershire to monitor incidents which involve alleged homosexual incidents, and again find that a lot of evidence of homosexual activity is based on hearsay rather than actual observed occurrence. In Hounslow the council have tried to address the issue of casual sex in parks by both homosexuals and heterosexuals—and the dangers of such encounters—by providing leaflets and engaging with people suspected of 'loitering' and talking to them about HIV/AIDs issues, as well as the possibility of physical assault.

Fears & mis-conceptions

All these discussions, evidence of patterns of use, and individual opinions, only confirm the centrality of parks to people's lives, even where there are conflicts of interest or expressions of antagonism or intolerance towards other people's concerns. Yet perhaps more than any other space or place in the modern town or city, it is the park which is most open to multiple uses, and to the widest range of groups and interests at different times of the day, week, season and year. It is the least regulated, the least ordered, administered and directed place, and as such, embodies all the attributes, good and bad, of individual freedom. However, as the urban designer Kevin Lynch once wrote, 'The controls and shapes that make space free are difficult to achieve and precarious to maintain.'

yes

Section VI A QUESTION OF MANAGEMENT

No statutory mandate   The provision of parks and open spaces by local authorities is a legal option rather than a statutory duty, although since so much open space was given in trust, there is an obligation to maintain it to a minimum standard. In an era of severe constraints on public spending, as Alan Barber noted in Working Paper 2, 'many councils take the simplistic view that statutory services take priority over non–statutory services.' Hence the slow but continuing reduction in spending on parks and open spaces. An added problem is that parks are not considered in the SSA (Standard Spending Assessment) which determines central government levels of financial support to individual local authorities, and therefore tend to get overlooked in local authority budgets and policies once again. On the other hand, there are strong arguments against including parks as statutory provision, as this might lead to notions of 'minimum levels' of spending on maintenance, which might then become the accepted norm.

Policies on parks   In 1994 the Audit Commission also conducted a survey of Parks and Open Spaces provided by London Boroughs, Metropolitan and District Councils in England and Wales. 178 (44%) of authorities responded. Among the self–reported findings were:

- Expenditure on parks had hardly changed since the 1988 survey—in effect 'a decrease in real terms'.

- 84% of expenditure on parks was on grounds maintenance contracts.

- Less than half of the authorities reported having security staff.

- Where local authorities had developed policies, these were much more likely to relate to questions of tree management, nature conservation or environmental issues, rather than to issues around park use, user likes and dislikes, safety or any other social issues.

- Toilets were provided in only about 30% of parks and open spaces; disabled toilets in less than 10% and refreshment kiosks in less than 10%.

- A high proportion of local authorities claim to involve residents in the management of parks.

- 52% of Metropolitan & London Boroughs say that there are formal arrangements for using volunteer staff.

- An average of just 1% of the staff budget is spent on staff training.

- A significant number of local authorities claimed to monitor the number of visits made to parks, and local surveys of 'satisfaction' produce satisfaction rates of approximately 75% of those asked.

While this survey provides much valuable information, some of the results should be regarded with a degree of scepticism, notably the claims for high levels of resident involvement in parks management, the use of volunteer help, and the high 'satisfaction' rates recorded in local surveys. This does not square with the evidence collected by many who have looked at local authority parks management closely.

One issue which we return to time and time again is the unequal balance between park maintenance and park development. Grounds maintenance is the name of the game as far as most parks policies are concerned at present. As David Welch, Director of the Royal Parks, has written, with regard to CCT contracts: 'The specifications that I have been asked to read and comment upon have contained few references to development work and the majority none at all. Development should be anticipated and written into the tender documents and remembered when annual estimates come around.'[34] In Hounslow a Landscape Development Team carries out major works distinct from Grounds Maintenance. But development means more than better landscaping and refurbished facilities; it also implies creating stronger links with users, and involving a wider range of people in the management policy of the park.

Maintenance or development?

Parks managers often complain, rightly in our opinion, that there are often double standards within Leisure Departments as to the quality of indoor and outdoor facilities. No indoor sports centre would be run with the low or non–existent staffing levels, filthy toilets, and lack of customer care that parks often exhibit, even though the parks may often account for as much use as the indoor centres. Yet attitudes here are changing. Central to this change of attitude has been the development of the idea of the park as being 'a leisure centre without a roof', strongly advocated across the board by officers in Middlesbrough's Leisure Services Department. They are moving towards a programme of management that regards indoor and outdoor facilities as equally deserving of the same qualities of management.

Double standards of leisure

This park was the focus of a successful £3m City Challenge bid by Middlesbrough Council, keen to renew facilities in the east of the town, and it won the ILAM 'Park of the Year' award in 1993. The scheme was based on renewing a run down Victorian park by locating a new leisure centre in the middle of it, with children's facilities, meeting rooms, cafe, indoor games area, and high quality changing room. The park is floodlit and open from 10am to 10pm every day. Outdoor facilities include a bowls green, five–a–side football and tennis courts, and a very large, imaginative and very popular children's play area. The park and the centre have a full–time management team, offering booking facilities, hire of rooms for children's parties and so on. In short, it is a properly run leisure centre. A limited observation exercise undertaken in the course of this study found, significantly, a higher number of women users, and a higher number than average of (accompanied) young babies.

PALLISTER PARK,
MIDDLESBROUGH

Lottery Money
Whether attitudes will change as a result of the sudden arrival of large amounts of lottery money remains to be seen. English Heritage have run at least one seminar on the implications of the Fund for park renewal, but at the time of writing the strict emphasis on capital expenditure on 'heritage' features, which is written into the criteria of the Fund, seems only to have produced schemes for re–instating or renewing traditional park railings and bandstands. Yet as the Public Prospects report graphically shows, simply lavishing large sums of money on restoring heritage features in heavily vandalised Victorian parks, without addressing the social context, could prove both short–sighted and wasteful. Lottery funding is addressed in the final section.

Strategic thinking
Yet all is not lost. Local authorities are beginning to develop strategic policies, and a number of the local authorities participating in the Comedia/Demos study have been developing parks strategies, often as part of wider leisure strategies. In Bristol the responsibility for parks and urban open spaces now lies within the remit of the Divisional Director of Community Initiatives, which as the name suggests, see parks management as being increasingly informed by the processes of community development, and based on local consultation. In Cardiff, the Council has produced a new strategy for leisure, 'The Future of Leisure in Cardiff', September 1994, in which parks and open spaces are seen as one of the five key leisure functions delineated in the strategy. Merton Council has drawn up historical and ecological management plans for three of their historic sites: Wimbledon Park (Grade II listed), John Innes Park and Morden Park.

Sheffield Council commissioned an independent consultant, Alan Barber, to produce a Sheffield Parks Regeneration Strategy which was published in 1993. Greenwich Council Leisure Services produced a Strategy for Parks and Open Space in 1991. Leicester has addressed the needs of public space in its 'Parks for People' policy. Hounslow has a Parks Strategy (1993) and a Green Strategy (1990). Perhaps the most active has been that developed by Bromley Leisure Services, where Committee approval has been given to re-distribute a large element of the general maintenance budget towards a particular network of prioritised parks, within a long term programme of rolling enhancement, district by district. In a sentence, the key element of the strategy is that, rather than generally maintain all of the parks and open spaces at a minimal level of improvement, it may be more beneficial to prioritise key parks (chosen in consultation with the public), to produce visible and evident improvements.

Should people pay?
As far as we know, the suggestion that people should pay to use parks (notably the more formal parks) is not widely expressed, but it certainly has now been made. In *Horticulture Week* John Fletcher made just such a case, claiming that:

'Introducing a small entrance charge for our city parks would:

- Reduce vandalism
- Increase standards of maintenance & facilities
- Provide a creative outlet for landscape designers
- Reduce local authority financial burden
- Provide better facilities for the disadvantaged
- Protect parks fallen into disrepair from re-development...'

John Fletcher, Horticulture Week (17/2/94)

While such an idea seems immediately attractive, it really doesn't bear much further scrutiny. For it is the intense and regular use made of parks by a loyal section of the community which would be mostly affected. And for most other people, it is precisely the 'free' (in all senses) nature of the public park that distinguishes it from the increasingly commercialised environment that is the modern city. Strong feelings were voiced in the Leicester interviews over the imposition of an entrance fee to Abbey Park for the Abbey Park Show, which was seen as taking away a public resource. Like the public library, the public park continues to represent a long–standing and different tradition of 'universal and lifelong' provision to that of the deliberately segmented and segmenting market–place.

On hearing about this study, a colleague wrote from Bologna in Italy where he and his family now lived, with an interesting comment on the issue of paying:

Paying in parks: a vignette (Bob Lumley)

'The contrast with British parks was interesting. In the Giardini Margherita (but also in the smaller parks) there were merry–go–rounds, miniature go–carts, trampolines, and (at weekends), tricycles and a toy train. At first, this was heaven. There were also some slides and climbing frames but they didn't compete well with the other things on offer. Later, our perception changed. The problem was simply the cost: one four–minute trip on the merry–go–round was 1,000 lire; multiply by two (children) and then by three for the number of trips, you'd spent the equivalent of £3; the trampoline was 5,000 lire for ten minutes. Net result: a visit to the Giardini Margherita cost about £5 a time. We discovered a lot of parents only went to the park on Saturdays because of the expense. That can't be right.'

YES

The general principle that public access should be free remains, it seems to us, unquestionable. However, people do expect to pay for some facilities within parks—tennis court charges, hire of boats on a boating lake, putting green fees, hire of pitches, special events and so on. This mixture of free access combined with some charged for facilities is well established in public parks. The question of how to develop the right mix of charged for and free facilities within the park seems more relevant. Good cafes and refreshment facilities can support park use. Similarly, high quality (floodlit) all–weather pitches or running tracks, which people (or clubs) pay to use, can, for example, encourage evening and winter use. Fairs, festivals and events are often paid for and these provide temporary commercial attractions within parks. As long as paid for services do not overwhelm the sense of parks as free public places, they can provide added attractions and positively encourage general park use. Leisure centres in Britain have become adept at using differential pricing and time tabling to encourage off–peak use. The programming of events and the charging policy for facilities in parks may also be used to similar effect.

Earning money The principle that charged for facilities should enhance and add to the overall offer of a park, can also be used to guide other methods of raising money. 'Income generation' should serve the greater good of the park and not be seen as a way of cutting costs. This means that all the money generated by a park should be invested back into the park. People might not resent paying for car–parking, for example, if they knew that the money collected was helping to pay for the park. Income generation may seem inimical to park use. However, improved catering, better parking, high quality pitches, bowling greens, sports facilities, events, specialist gardens and even garden nurseries and other building based facilities, can (where appropriate) contribute to parks by providing additional attractions.

The challenge of CCT The Local Government Planning and Land Act 1980 introduced CCT (Compulsory Competitive Tendering) to local government services. In 1988 the Local Government Act extended this requirement to include grounds maintenance and the management of sports and leisure facilities. To date it would appear that CCT has largely meant cheaper grounds maintenance contracts, but the savings are often lost to parks department budgets, and public concerns for safety and supervision as a result remain largely unmet. A survey conducted by the London Boroughs Association in 1994 into the effects of CCT on parks found that 'most boroughs stated that where savings had been made they were normally released to the centre.'[35] In other words the borough treasurer had reaped the benefits of savings made through competition, rather than the parks service being allowed to use the money saved to re–invest.

> **Cemetery Manager on the effect of CCT** *They asked me what was required and I gave them full details. They haven't acted on all of it or very little of it. As far as they're concerned they treat the cemetery as a park which is, go in on a machine, cut it, and go out again'.* [36]

The effects of CCT Another survey of the effects of CCT undertaken by Bill Swan, an MSc student in the Department of Horticulture at the University of Reading, found that average local authority savings as a result of CCT were 16% but, 'in the majority (66%) of authorities, none of this was made available to parks.' Although CCT had brought clear benefits to many parks in terms of higher levels of specification for maintenance, there was one area where there was widespread concern, and that was to do with public perceptions of staffing and safety. The survey asked whether local authorities had received public reports of a perceived increase or decrease in informal policing/presence in parks by grounds staff since the introduction of CCT, and 'of those able to comment, the vast majority reported a decrease—most notably authorities with denser urban populations.'

The impact of CCT has largely resulted in on–site staff being replaced **The keeper–less park?** by mobile contractors and security services. Yet rather than creating a greater feeling of safety in parks, it seems that mobile security staff can be seen to signal danger. The paradox that the presence of uniformed security staff—with all the paraphernalia of vans, dogs and mobile phones—may exacerbate public unease, is a lesson for our times. The public disillusion with existing models of park security seems widespread and immensely damaging, as we have reported. As was made evident in the Reading survey, CCT has created a feeling among the public that staff have disappeared. A senior parks manager in Westminster said that,

> 'The lack of staff presence in parks is the main reason for the decline in public open space and parks ... The division of responsibilities between duties of roving gangs of bonus–oriented 'grounds maintenance operatives', park police and litter removers makes no one ultimately responsible for any aspect. In my opinion, the presence of patrol staff/skilled gardeners who are allocated to particular areas is the foundation stone of good park management.'[37]

Certainly during the observation exercises, researchers were astonished to realise that during the course of a day in which as many as a thousand people visited some of the parks, there was never a keeper or staff member to be seen in some of them. The 'keeper–less park' has joined the driver–less train, the unstaffed railway station, the unsupervised playground or underground car park, as one of the ghostly sites of public Britain.

However most new thinking about parks management has been **Parks police** around security issues, and, rather worryingly, a popular line of thought—certainly in London—seems to be for a more para–military, vehicle–based, 'law and order' approach. This could be short–termism. In August 1994, Wandsworth Council applied to the Home Office for permission to extend its parks police force, so that they could also patrol on a number of housing estates and other areas of council property. Parks police, who are sworn in by magistrates, enjoy special legislation giving some of them limited powers of arrest. Greenwich Council is now experimenting with a Parks Police scheme, though much less extensive in its powers. There are other approaches to the issue of public security, and it is worth bearing in mind what the philosopher Sir Karl Popper said on this question: 'We must plan for freedom and not only for security, if for no other reason than that only freedom can make security secure.' But this is not just a matter of the finer points of liberal philosophy; practice shows that there are more benign forms of policing by community involvement and natural surveillance.

THE SAFER PARKS
PROJECT

> Hartlepool is the home of Britain's first Safer Parks Project, set up by a local community activist with support from Hartlepool Council and the local TEC (Training & Enterprise Council) as a training programme. It arose out of very real local concern that some parks were becoming so vandalised, and perceived to be so unsafe, that people had stopped using them. Marney Harris, the Safer Parks Co-ordinator, says that it is greater use and community involvement in parks that is the key to public safety. 'We tried increased security but it wasn't enough'. What did work was an increase in events and activities in parks organised by local groups.

A different kind
of security

In the course of the study researchers visited the Phoenix community garden near Charing Cross Road in central London, developed by voluntary local labour from an abandoned car park. It now receives a small grant from Camden Council. The park, which is very small, but beautifully landscaped and planted, with a pond and children's sandpit, is in the heart of an area with a large number of homeless people, drunks and late night clubbers. It is never locked. Yet they claim to have few security problems. During the visit the part–time woman gardener was observed to stop off from her work for a moment to walk over and politely ask a small group of young men—who came in to sit on a bench to roll a cannabis 'joint'—to leave, and did the same later to a drunk clutching a can of beer who staggered in, and then staggered out. Both exchanges were conducted in a friendly but firm way, and both were extremely successful. There was no 'macho' stand–off, no calling for reinforcements or for the police. There may be a lesson here for understanding a different kind of public security.

Women in
management

Of the many questions raised by this small vignette, two are particularly worth highlighting: the role of women in parks management, and community 'ownership', both of which are highly germane to the security issue. Firstly it has to be asked why women are so poorly represented in senior parks management in Britain, and yet they have played such an important role in private gardening, horticulture and landscape architecture. Martin Hoyles in Working Paper 6, has pointed to the long tradition of women gardeners and horticulturists. As is clear from this study, while some of the most trenchant and informed critiques of public space design and provision have been made by women—for example, Jacquie Burgess, Hazel Conway, Judy Hillman, Susan Lasdun, Doreen Massey, Janice Morphet, Hilary Taylor, and Elizabeth Wilson— this involvement has largely not been reflected at the level of management and policy, although women are increasingly being found in senior management positions within Leisure Departments. It is salutary to remember that in North America, women have taken the lead in a number of the most well known parks renewal projects: the Director of Central Park, New York, and the person most responsible for its renewed status is Elizabeth Barlow Rogers, along with Linda Davidoff, Executive Director of the Parks Council, New York. Julia Sniderman, Preservation & Planning Supervisor, Chicago Parks District, USA has also been influential in park regeneration programmes. The definitive history of American parks has been written by Galen Cranz and she continues to influence policies for parks.

Questions of consultation and a sense of ownership of public spaces are also now at issue. Some case studies have shown that the culture of consultation is too limited—and in some cases non–existent within local authority processes, despite the findings of the Audit Commission survey. Yet parks are emerging as a key local site of disputes about authority (the Sheffield Save Our Parks campaign, for example), and parks are also a site for community development, as our own case studies in Bristol and Sutton have shown. Part of the above process will involve deciding who has the moral and emotional ownership of public space, and how can it be 'policed' by consensus and the development of public trust, an issue dealt with by Jacquie Burgess in Working Paper 8. In many ways the park represents a testing ground for the issues of community self–management and stewardship.

The culture of consultation

Many parks and open spaces are now caught between the contradictory plans and purposes of both providers and users. As has been shown in many of the interviews and discussion groups, most people still think that it is 'their' (the local authority's) job to provide, fund and manage parks, while the local authorities are seeking to devolve some sense of management and custody to the community. But neither side is handling the arrangement very well, it seems. At the heart of this confusion is the question of symbolic ownership. Is it the local authority which 'owns' the park, because of its legal land entitlements, its elected accountability, its professional staffing and so on, or is it the community which actually lives by the park, uses it, and pays national and local taxes to ultimately fund it? Unless some body or group of people feels a direct sense of ownership, then the park is unlikely to prosper. The Bristol case study showed that sensitive community development can bring about much stronger feelings of ownership of parks and open spaces, which in turn generates a stronger sense of community and local identity.

A sense of ownership

From the same city of Bologna as the story about the commercial children's play area, comes a different story: about how an old people's centre took over the management of a park that was in decline and turned it into a centre of popular cultural activity:

*An example from Italy
(Lia Ghilardi)*

> 'Santa Viola is part of Reno, one of 9 districts of the city of Bologna. Reno has 32,300 inhabitants, a quarter of which live in S. Viola, a traditionally working–class area, whose residents are still mostly skilled workers. The population comprises a strong southern Italian immigrant community, most of whom came to Bologna in search of work in the late fifties, and settled in S. Viola because of the area's proximity to factories. They are now totally integrated and take an active part in the life

and activities of the neighbourhood. Of the 11,300 inhabitants of S. Viola, 3,600 are retired (aged over 60).

'In S. Viola the old people organise themselves on a voluntary basis and carry out not only recreational activities but also organise community education programmes, linking their activities to the local schools and the library. Up to the mid eighties, S. Viola had relatively few green spaces and only one small run–down park, which had become a meeting point for drug users, and which is situated in between two estates. As soon as the old people's centre was opened, the park was immediately identified as a target for regeneration. In conjunction with the local sports centre (run by local residents and built by local residents with the local authority putting in only the money for construction materials), a series of initiatives such as 'Green Saturdays' and park and open spaces 'Cleaning–Up days' were started which involved schools, residents and young drug addicts.

'To fund the 'Open Spaces Cleaning–Up Days' money was raised by a photographic exhibition documenting the history of the community, using photographs, many of which dated back to the beginning of this century, provided by the old people who had grown up near those open spaces. Then specific days were declared Cleaning–Up Days. During these, three run–down open spaces were identified and, with the help of two skilled gardeners living in the neighbourhood, these areas were turned into gardens and herb gardens where today schoolchildren keep plants and experiment with cross–fertilisation of flowers and plants. A large section of the local population participated in Cleaning–Up Days.

'The park today has tables for card playing (weather permitting), a space for open–air performances (usually singing and dancing competitions organised by the old people's centre), a jogging track, a cycle way where the disabled can safely be trained to use wheelchairs, and where small children can learn to cycle. Women are involved not only in the upkeep of the gardens and the park, but also in the supervision of these areas, which is done in regular daily shifts. (Until now the issue of safety has been dealt with by groups of elderly women who are known in the area and who seem to know everybody.) Today, the park is seen as an invaluable resource of well–being by all sectors of the community.'

An example from Sheffield

Hillsborough Park has recently been the focus of a renewal programme organised by a new local charity, the Hillsborough Community Development Trust. They have reclaimed a walled garden and with an estimated 12,000 hours of voluntary effort have created a community garden, part of which is dedicated as a memorial to those who died in the Hillsborough disaster of 1989. A similar project to create a park to commemorate a local tragedy happened in Dublin where the Stardust Memorial Park was created close to the site of a dance hall which caught fire one night, and in which 48 young people died. This links to a long tradition of Remembrance and Memorial Gardens.

Questions of representation

Issues of consultation and representation are fraught with problems, and not all community initiatives will be as successful as the Bologna example cited above. Many parks do have 'Friends' groups or 'user' groups, but these in themselves may not necessarily be representative

of all local interests, for the concerns and interests of local house–
owners, dog–owners, Sunday footballers, teenage groups, festival or-
ganisers, advocates of night–time floodlit pitches, parents with young
children are not always compatible. Public consultation, like public
meetings, can quickly be hi–jacked by the most vociferous and best   YES
–organised groups.

But this does not mean that the commitment to widening debate
about, and 'ownership' of, local services and facilities should be abandoned. Demos has been a keen advocate of new kinds of consultation,
using citizens' juries and other local forums for power–sharing and
widening civic responsibility. Community development work undertaken by the parks service in Bristol has been a painful, protracted, but
occasionally very successful experiment in building coalitions of local
interests around parks issues. In this search for widening participation
in local decision–making, parks services are neither necessarily in front
of, or behind, any other institution, organisation or public body.

All these difficulties point to the urgent need for new management and   **New management &**
professional skills. The strongest tradition within parks management   **professional skills**
was until quite recently the horticultural tradition, but with the turn to
more ecological thinking in the planning of open green space, the privatisation of grounds maintenance, and the renewed concern for the
social and urban regeneration role of parks, new skills, particularly
'facility management' skills are clearly needed. The new links between
parks and other areas of urban policy, which in turn will require new
thinking about training and professional skills, are developed in the
following section.

Section VII NEW PERSPECTIVES

We began this study by asking the question, 'What is the rationale for urban parks in the late 1990s?' It is a serious question based on the acknowledgement that many public parks in Britain are clearly in desperate decline. This decline can be attributed to poor management and dwindling funds, but it is also in part the result of a failure of development and a lack of innovation in adapting different kinds and models of parks and open space to meet the needs of modern urban life. As we say in the introduction to this report, the public park is largely an urban invention, set up as a counterpoint to urban characteristics of density, the street form, and the intensity of the work place. Parks and cities go together. The Victorians imposed a very strong model of the public park, one which said much about their vision of society and the way people in cities—the new urban public—should behave. The link the Victorians made between public places and the nature of urban society is still accurate. What goes on in parks is a reflection or a symptom of changes in the wider urban society. Public parks reflect the ways in which the management and control of cities, and the ways people live their lives in them, are changing.

In this report we've pointed to the changes in city development, leisure lifestyles, patterns of work and city management. The capacity for local authorities to continue to pay for and manage the infrastructure of the public provision, first laid down by the Victorians in the early part of the century and expanded upon until the late 1970s, is now being seriously questioned. Victorian authorities and philanthropists spent substantial sums of money laying out and maintaining public parks with high horticultural and landscape standards. It is very likely that the relative amounts of money spent on individual public parks has declined since the early part of the century. Indeed the over the last 20 years urban local authorities have tended to acquire more open spaces while the money available to manage them has decreased. The first and most obvious sign of declining maintenance funds is the loss of staff from parks. As many people pointed out to us, in the course of survey work in many different parks, 'the park keeper has gone'.

Managing decline　It is arguable that over the last 20 years local authorities have largely been managing the decline of the Victorian park model. Many would argue that all that is needed is money to pay for higher maintenance, better quality horticulture and greater security. This may be true, but it is not at all obvious that more money would answer all the questions about the management and use of modern public parks. Although there have been innovations with city farms, community gardens and adventure playgrounds, public parks have not been substantially rethought in the light of the needs and changes in the modern city.

This failure is particularly serious in the context of local government finance where tough decisions have to be taken on expenditure. Politicians and other decision makers have very little information about the contemporary use and value of parks that they can draw on to inform and support any decisions in favour of spending money on parks. At the moment, the framework for evaluating the management of parks is a crude financial one. A good parks manager is one who can save money, a bad manager is one who overspends on the budget. There are very few ways in which he or she can demonstrate the positive value of parks and prove that parks are achieving important objectives in improving the quality of urban life, or indeed, ways of showing that a park has singularly failed to make a contribution to the life of an area.

Local authorities need to understand how their parks are used, they also need a framework within which to make rational decisions about expenditure, staffing and other kinds of investment. They need to understand how the larger infrastructure of open space is working in their areas, and how it fits into the urban fabric. Is it accessible? How is it used? The definitions used to define and plan for maintenance need to be more varied, flexible and responsive to the differences of use in particular localities. There is potential for a range of different kinds of places, some linking up areas of the city and providing new networks, canal walks, greenways and other ways of connecting up areas within the city. (This kind of 'park system' is increasingly common in German and Dutch approaches to city planning.) Other parks may be fenced off, enclosed areas within the city. Some parks may be better used for active pursuits, or as sites for new buildings, others may be managed for more passive uses. Yet other areas can be left as open and 'unplanned'. Of course these uses cannot be over prescribed or in anyway zoned. One of the strengths of public parks is the mix between non–instrumental and organised use, the conflict between different groups of users is in some ways an inevitable aspect of urban life and not always a bad thing. However, in some instances completely new models of open space, leisure gardens, school gardens, areas for food production and places with more ecological functions may be appropriate.

Not Bugg thrugh?

New approaches to parks must also encourage new and different kinds of ownership, or co–management arrangements between groups of organisations or local authorities and other parties. A more diverse mix of ownership and management arrangements can only help to encourage innovation and allow for different kinds of parks to develop.

A framework or strategy for open space will also allow local authorities to make more considered decisions for building, or selling some areas of open space which are redundant or unused. The quality of public space is as important as the quantity. The defence of all urban open space regardless of quality or use, reflects a deep sense of distrust and a failure of management. The view that protection of all open space is of the highest priority is a negative view both of urban life and of the capacity of cities to evolve and change.

In this section we put forward new perspectives for urban parks which help to construct contemporary rationales and argue for the social use of parks, the important relationship between parks and health, the potential for public parks within the emerging policies for Agenda 21 and re–thinking the role of parks in relation to planning. The question of radically improving urban parks is not simply answered by spending more money; there is now an urgent need for innovation, for a better understanding of the current role of parks, and for more insight into the potential of parks to meet new needs thrown up by modern urban life.

NEW PERSPECTIVES: SOCIAL

For too long the parks 'crisis' has involved users and providers, metaphorically, standing in the middle of a vandalised park or bereft green open space, and asking, 'what went wrong?' The next question then becomes, 'what needs to happen to make this space work again?' Often, without any consumer research, or in–depth and slow, patient consultation, large sums of money are spent re–equipping the children's playground, planting some more trees, mending the paths and fences, only to find that the equipment, planting and fences, are damaged or even destroyed once again. The starting point surely should be not *What does this park need to make it work again?*, but *What kinds of facilities does this neighbourhood need to become a viable neighbourhood or community?* Only part of the answer—and perhaps some times no part of the answer—might be a park.

Parks & the social agenda It should not be forgotten that Victorian parks were invariably part of a wider social agenda, and were premised on improving the moral and physical health of the urban poor. Yet the social agenda can conflict with other interests as has been observed. When George Lansbury was First Commissioner of Works in the first Labour government, he courted great unpopularity by his 'controversial drive to make the over–regulated Royal Parks of London fit for popular use'. He declared war on 'Keep off the Grass' notices, arguing that, 'Grass was made for man, not man for grass'. A programme of sports activities, running tracks, paddling pools and lidos, pageants and dancing areas, was instituted and was very popular with the working classes, but less so with traditional middle class park users. The Times called Lansbury, 'The Caliban of Parks', and there was vehement opposition to paddling pools and running tracks in Regent's Park by middle class house owners who regarded the park as an extension of their own homes and gardens. Lansbury's son recalled the sense of injustice felt by those who felt it unfair 'that 'paddly pools', running tracks, swings, see-saws, and other contraptions should be provided free of charge so that the ragamuffins from the slums of Camden Town and St Pancras might share the spaciousness, the cleanliness and the fresh air of the west side of the park.' [38]

In Boston, parks and open spaces were included in the city's anti–poverty initiative. Six main reasons for this were given:

Low–income people were most dependent on the public realm for relaxation, exercise, finding companionship and contact with nature;

Parks in poorer areas have historically received less maintenance, programming and capital investment;

A sense that degraded environments contributed to feelings of hopelessness and powerlessness on the part of inner city residents;

Urban parks were one of the few issues that brought people from different racial, ethnic and economic sectors together;

The rehabilitation of a park or community garden provided opportunities for grassroots leadership to emerge;

The problem of improving the quality of urban parks was seen as a problem that could be 'solved', in contrast to so many other seemingly intractable problems.

PARKS AND ANTI–POVERTY STRATEGIES

Source: Renaissance of an Urban Park System: The Boston Story. Mark Primack, Executive Director, Boston GreenSpace Alliance

There have been other visions since. When George Chadwick concluded his magisterial study of *The Park and the Town* in 1966, he allowed himself to imagine the developments which might come next.

Lost visions

'It follows thus that the new equivalent (of the traditional Victorian park) will have many and varied uses to serve and express; the possibilities are therefore richer, more diverse. Of specialised buildings, cafes, inns, libraries, museums, art galleries, nursery schools, swimming pools, gymnasia, theatres, dance halls, cinemas, meeting places, open and covered, of all kinds, may be met with.'

Chadwick was clearly still writing under the influence of the Festival of Britain and that kind of social democratic modernism which still prevailed, when the future was still a matter of possibility, of making it new, rather than the era of nostalgia for a lost past, which it became.

Another powerful voice at this time was that of the theatre director Joan Littlewood, who also had her vision of a new kind of park:

'I wanted a Vauxhall Gardens of today. I called it a fun palace to provoke people: but in Vauxhall Gardens from Pepys's time to the Industrial Revolution they had hot–air balloons, scientific lectures, they had Mrs Siddons (the tragic actress), they had ad–lib music and there was no class there, you could be with a whore or with milady. When I used to walk alone as a kid around the South Bank, I thought one day I will tear all this down and have it like it was at the time of Bankside. But I didn't get it, I didn't win.'

But this does not mean that such visions cannot be revived. If Britain's renewal is to involve universal child–care provision, investment in health, leisure, and in lifelong learning, then urban parks could well be the place to site these new ventures in social renewal.

Buildings in parks

For parks are obvious places in which to site children's nurseries, kindergartens and playgroups; some London parks still retain vestiges of the One O'Clock Clubs and other earlier manifestations of these facilities. In Bromley by Bow, a community organisation has taken over the management of the local park from Tower Hamlets Council, and is planning to site the new health centre building in the park, with doors and a cafe/seating area, looking out across the flower beds and lawns. Surely this is better than siting a new health centre in a busy street? Wandsworth Council have restored the traditional Pump House in Battersea Park and converted it into an art gallery, with a shop and information centre. Battersea Park is also the home of the magnificent 1985 Peace Pagoda, a 38–foot high pagoda based on traditional Indian and Japanese designs and donated to the park by the Japanese Buddhist Order, Nipponzan Myohoji. It has not been vandalised at all, and adds a distinct and unique feature to the park and sky–line. Two of Merton's leisure centres are based in parks. In 1995 crafts and arts studios will be opened to the public in the newly restored Victorian stable block in Redlees Park. In Middlesbrough, there is an ambitious plan to link the Dorman Museum with Albert Park, to create an integrated space and set of facilities, where at present the two places are simply adjacent without any linkages. The modern swimming pool and children's playground, located in Highbury Fields, ideally suits the site and surroundings. In Glasgow, there is a proposal to re-create the 1930's Tait Tower and Palace of Arts in Bellahouston Park.

Protected from ourselves?

To advocate such facilities does not mean not acknowledging some of the problems. The escalating cost of maintaining paddling pools, for example, under modern Health & Safety legislation, is tending to become prohibitive, involving as it does daily cleaning and staffing requirements that local authorities can no longer afford. Food and hygiene legislation has increased the costs of running any kind of catering facility in a park. These new forms of legislation, while admirable in intention, seem now to be in danger of preventing the very kind of amenable and impromptu social life that they may have been intended to promote.

Such focal points of interest bring new visitors and users to parks; and busier parks are perceived to be safer parks. Yet many of the most innovative new buildings and facilities are being sited and developed in city farms, or ecology gardens, managed and maintained by voluntary organisations. Why has it been left to the voluntary sector to commission exciting new buildings such as energy–efficient study centres (Islington Ecology Centre based on a piece of wasteland) or the proposed sustainable visitor centre for Kirkby urban farm in Liverpool designed by Baker–Brown McKay Sustainable Design, while local authorities lose their nerve even about building new toilet blocks or refurbishing out–dated cafe buildings and kiosks? Is it just money?

NEW PERSPECTIVES: HEALTH

The association between urban parks and good public health was estab-   Parks and public health
lished in the way the Victorians first made the case for public parks partly in terms of reducing urban overcrowding and disease, although the early arguments were as much about public morals as they were about public health. The link between green open space and the public health has continued to be made, albeit in very general terms. The precise health benefits and specific arguments that demonstrate the health benefits of public parks have not been made.

The relationship between public parks and public health is an important perspective for the future development of urban parks. This is not an opportunistic link, but reflects the growing convergence between leisure, health and urban policy. The Department of Environment report *Assessing the Impact of Urban Policy*, published in 1994 reviews the approach and effect of the last 10 years of urban policy initiatives including programmes such as Action for Cities, Urban Priority Areas, Housing Investment Programmes and Urban Programme Funding. As part of this review a residents' survey was carried out and this showed that health care was second behind violent crime, on the list of factors affecting their lives. The report concluded that given the importance residents attach to health care it is surprising that health has not featured as one of the formal elements of urban policy.[39] The London Borough of Southwark held a conference in 1994 bringing together health professionals and parks and leisure managers to explore the relationship between public parks and urban health policies.

History, size and situation of the park in the city   THE SENSUAL EXPERIENCE OF
On a site that had become derelict and was formerly used for mining and   THE 'HEALTHPARK
manufacturing the city of Bottrop developed a varied concept for recreation and   QUELLENBUSCH' IN BOTTROP
smaller enterprises. The area spans 40 ha. within a regional green belt around
the cities of Oberhausen, Mühlheim, and Bottrop. Some 10 ha. provides the   *Ralf Ebert, Working Paper 12*
core of the Healthpark Quellenbusch, between the hospital of Bottrop and the
district–park Vonderort.

Concept
The Healthpark creates a design that allows new 'sensual experiences'. It
supports general healthcare, rehabilitation, and self–help groups. A health
centre is being built, with a multi–purpose sports hall, health care and catering
arrangements. Alongside sporting activities there will be saunas, hydropathic
baths and alternative therapies. A perfumed garden is planned, as well as space
for meditation, a gymnastics area and a tropical environment. Wherever
possible open green spaces and fallow areas are to be left in their natural state.
Natural therapies are to be encouraged through the open spaces in the park
The experience of quietness, enclosure and safety is a way for people to
address their illnesses and create a positive attitude towards life. The park is
open to the general public for recreation and leisure.

Pollution   Current public health pre–occupations include the effects of traffic pollution, sedentary lifestyles, the effects of poor diets, mental health problems, the spread of viruses, HIV infection, poverty and stress. Air pollution in cities is widely recognised as an urban health threat and the case for parks and green space in ameliorating pollution is part of a wider environmental debate. The health hazards inside buildings are also beginning to be understood. A recent article in the Lancet points out that city dwellers spend 90% of their time in buildings and that pollutants inside can be much worse than those outside. [40] Air conditioning, central heating, and toxic materials can all be detrimental to health. Outdoor places such as parks might well provide relief from indoor pollution. Perhaps ironically, research undertaken at Heston Park in Hounslow, despite being close to the Heathrow flight path, found that the park was considered a place for peace and quiet.

Source: Dr Martyn Partridge,
Chief Medical Adviser,
National Asthma Campaign.

> The asthma epidemic of June 1994 caused 'a rush of extra patients equivalent to a plane crash near every hospital over a wide area of southern and central England'. Health professionals believe it resulted from a combination of traffic fumes and unusual weather conditions. One in seven children now suffers from asthma, and in some city centres the figure is one in three.

Exercise   The National Fitness Survey produced by the Sports Council and the Health Education Authority in 1992 showed that the majority of people surveyed did not take the exercise necessary to achieve a health benefit.[41] The value of exercise is reflected in the emergence of schemes whereby doctors recommend and even prescribe exercise to some patients. Birmingham's 'Exercise on Prescription Scheme' was launched in 1994. They have four Health and Fitness advisers working with 33 GPs. The posts were funded in part by the Regional Health Authority and the Family Health programme. The advisers have set up walking groups and running groups. Medical staff stress that exercise does not necessarily mean sport, but can mean simple activities such as fast walking and cycling. In his paper written for this study, Mike Collins points out that while participants in formal organised sports are a minority of park users, much higher numbers of people use parks to play informal games. Mike Collins predicts an increase in demand for sports facilities and points to growing numbers of women and older people taking up informal sports. [42] At the moment much of the 'exercise on prescription' activity takes place in leisure centres. It could take place in parks, if more attention were given to the management and provision of appropriate facilities.

Psychological   The effects of nature on people's psychological state of mind is beginning to be researched. Although at early stages, studies are claiming to show a range of benefits from relieving mental fatigue, effecting mood changes and relaxation as a result of looking at or experiencing 'natural' landscapes.[43] In general, mental health is recognised as a major contemporary health issue. The Lancet article argues that mental well–being is a neglected aspect of city life and that just as infectious diseases were confronted with public health measures 200 years ago, dealing with mental illnesses must now be part of urban health programmes. Horticultural therapy schemes have become established and there is now a national organisation promoting them. Many schemes involve people with depression or learning difficulties who gain benefits from tending plants. Apart from the horticultural therapy project in Battersea park in London, most of these projects have been set up in botanical gardens, community gardens and city farms. New health centres and hospitals pay much more attention to the quality of the grounds and gardens. In Hounslow, Acton Lodge secured a European Grant to develop a project with adults with learning difficulties to reclaim and use the disused nursery site in Chiswick House Grounds. The Royal Brompton National Heart and Lung Hospital in Chelsea have built a garden for the relaxation of patients and staff. The Bromley by Bow Centre will create a new garden to complement the Health Centre.

Addressing questions of mental health in the city implies taking a broader social perspective. Such an approach was pioneered by a group of doctors in the 1920s who attempted to study the conditions (social, personal, physical and psychological) of health. The doctors argued then, that 'health' was more than the absence of disease and disorder, and that health had to be actively striven for. They set up the Peckham Health Centre, a kind of health and social centre, and found that factors such as relationships, friendships, networks of support, the availability of good child care, affected people's sense of well–being and their health.[44] A more recent study in the USA by the Department of Parks and Recreation of the Pennsylvania State University found that people perceived the benefits of parks as related to exercise, relaxation and peace. The study found that personal benefits brought about by parks had a strong health and wellness bias, and concluded that the value of parks was understood as primarily providing benefits for people, rather than providing environmental and conservation benefits. The authors argued that while local recreation and park agencies are only beginning to think of themselves as 'health' or 'wellness' organisations, the public already does so. [45]

Social

There are four cities designated as healthy cities under the World Health Organisation programme (Belfast, Glasgow, Liverpool, Camden). The 'healthy cities' movement emerged from the World Heath Organisation's 'Health for All' programme, which began as a global strategy. Since 1987 the 'Health for All' network has been concerned with public participation, interagency partnership, tackling inequality and developing a social vision of health that is reminiscent of the model pioneered by the Peckham experiment. 'Healthy Sheffield' was set up as a result of collaboration between eight organisations in the city. Healthy Sheffield has produced a city health plan that refers to the use and access to greenspace and recreation. In general, the Healthy Cities programmes mention the importance of open space and access

Healthy Cities

to the countryside, but do not refer specifically to the role or potential of urban parks in cities.

There are many ways in which urban parks could contribute to the health of the city. The Comedia surveys showed that about 70% of those interviewed said they walked to their parks. In the light of concerns about urban traffic and people's lack of exercise, this fact alone begins to demonstrate the potential value of public parks. A significant section of those interviewed (around 30% in some London parks) said they did not take trips to the countryside. For these people, urban parks are the only green spaces they have ready access to. In terms of the psychological benefits, people involved in the study have described the contemplative, almost private and personal uses of parks. People go to talk, or when depressed, or to gain a sense of personal freedom. These uses can be seen as part of the wider social benefits of parks.

NEW PERSPECTIVES: PLANNING

Parks and urban planning

Is there a case for arguing that the government should issue planning policy guidance for parks? We have argued that the current planning definitions can be too reductive and that they concentrate on the quantitative questions of open space provision at the expense of qualitative issues. During this study, some local authority Councillors have expressed frustration at the rigidity of land use designations for parks and open space that can be used to prevent any kind of development, even that designed to enhance the use of the park. However, in Janice Morphet's view the protection afforded to existing open spaces has been reduced over the last fifteen years, although she too states that the current approach to open space within the planning system is confused and under–informed. Would policy guidance for urban parks help to explore the relationship between planning policies and other development policies or would it work to further reinforce the existing land use designations?

Janice Morphet identifies the *creation* of new open space and the *protection* of existing open space as the two key issues for planning policy. A Planning Policy Guideline (PPG) for urban parks may help to elaborate policy for these issues and provide a framework to help guide the difficult question of when disposal of open space might be appropriate.

The provision for outdoor sport and recreation is recognised in PPG17 '*Sport and Recreation*', published in 1991. The PPG has been useful in helping authorities to evaluate the need for open space and to consider open space alongside other development issues. However, these guidance notes have also been criticised for an over reliance on quantitative standards, again at the expense of qualitative questions that reflect the distinctive character of different localities. The PPG17 was written before the Rio Summit and therefore doesn't reflect the more recent concerns about sustainable development and the growing emphasis on the need to develop more liveable cities.

Extract from a speech given by Tony Baldry Parliamentary Under Secretary of State, to the NPFA 26/4/93.

'One of the keys to achieving sustainable development will be to make our cities more liveable. In other words, we must make adequate provision for development. But we must also ensure that urban amenities and environmental quality are maintained and improved.

In this way we can pass on to the next generation, cities that have a better environment and better recreation facilities than we inherited. Open space must play an important role. As a Minister responsible for planning, I see creating liveable cities as a major challenge for the planning system. We must ensure that there is sufficient open space, of the right sort, in the right place. '

A PPG for parks and open space could take up the challenge set by Tony Baldry and provide a framework for the protection, creation and disposal of open space, that recognises questions of quality, value and diversity, and sets urban parks within the wider context of creating liveable cities that put people's needs first. A PPG on parks and open spaces could complement existing guidance on sport and recreation and guidance on enhancing the viability and vitality of town centres. Together this planning advice can start to address major questions of urban policy and how to improve life in cities.

Cultural planning

In urban renewal strategies, parks can be of vital importance. In Barcelona's renewal in the 1980s—partly in readiness for the Olympic Games—the Public Works Department decided on a programme to 'open up' the city with a phased programme of creating small pocket parks and small plazas, concentrating on the hidden historic areas of the city, and derelict spaces. By 1991 200 parks had been created or were in the process of being so, with artists as central figures in the design teams.

'In Barcelona, the Parc Crueta dell Coll at the furthest part of the city from the sea is a new lido carved out from an old quarry. Sculptures by the American artist Ellsworth Kelly create the dramatic gateway to the park, and a huge crab-like concrete sculpture by Catalan artist Eduardo Chillida makes an extraordinary centre–piece over the lake. The Parc de l'Esacio del Nord is a huge expanse where disused railway sheds and a station are being converted into a new cultural centre, and the landscape of the park is itself an environmental sculpture by American artist Beverley Pepper. Trees planted in a whirlpool formation, and hillocks for children to skate and cycle on, are decorated with ceramics in a tribute to Gaudi and Miro.'[46]

Much of the most interesting new art in Britain is sculptural, architectural and concerned with natural landscaping, notably in the work of Andy Goldsworthy and Richard Long. There are clearly opportunities for parks to become the sites of new artistic landscaping features, and already a number of parks have used artists to help them design new features and facilities.

*Fran Cottell, Visual Arts Co-
ordinator, Merton Council*

> 'In the London Borough of Merton we are now (1994) developing a green arts policy where artworks often involve devising concepts for parks and school playgrounds; tree planting, water features and landscape where appropriate can be drawn into plans for primarily sculptural seating and wall–painting artworks.'

NEW PERSPECTIVES: AGENDA 21

Agenda 21: an
opportunity

Agenda 21 presents another important (perhaps all embracing) perspective from which to work out new approaches to the development and management of urban parks. Agenda 21 is the name of the programme of action for achieving more sustainable forms of development agreed at the 1992 'Earth Summit' in Rio de Janeiro. The notion of community involvement to deliver this agenda was encapsulated by the following understanding: 'By 1996 most local authorities in each country should have undertaken a consultative process with their populations and achieved a consensus on a 'Local Agenda 21' for the community'. Since Rio, the Local Agenda 21 process has proved, certainly in the UK, to be the principal vehicle for implementing Agenda 21. Over 50% of local authorities in the UK are now committed to drawing up their own action plans for LA21. The Local Government Management Board is currently engaged in 6 pilot studies.

Working together

As presently understood, sustainability largely means new ways of thinking about the efficient and less wasteful use of natural and material resources; of reducing environmental pollution; of protecting natural diversity; of creating decent jobs, homes, educational prospects for everybody; for creating viable settlements and communities. However, Agenda 21 is not just concerned with the environment but *how environmental, economic and social issues interact and can be made to work together for the common good*. Whilst it recognises that sustainable development is primarily the responsibility of governments it also acknowledges that it will only work if it encourages broad public participation and the active involvement of non–governmental organisations and other groups. Community consultation and the involvement of organisations outside the local authority are particularly relevant for the future management of public parks.

Social sustainability

To date, though, the emphasis has been on thinking about—and acting upon—ecological and environmental sustainability. However, if these issues are to be fully developed, wider questions of the quality of social relationships, questions of common belief systems and patterns of trust, of notions of citizenship and voluntary activity, of organisational capacity and social capital, have to be put at the heart of the Agenda 21 process.

The role of parks

Public parks, their current use and the potential they have for community activity and environmental projects have not really been included in the emerging Agenda 21 debate and this exclusion is a matter of concern. This study suggests that they (and allotments and cemeteries) should be brought into the definition of sustainability, and need to be recognised as sites for community activity and should form part of any set of indicators developed to measure sustainability.

Long–term improvements of urban parks are more likely to occur as the result of alliances between local authorities and local organisations, groups and individuals. Encouraging groups from outside local authorities to influence the development of parks can help to build up positive pressure for change. The energy and momentum for massively improving the parks in Boston came from an alliance of groups and interests, who, together, became a formidable force, generating investment funds and re–defining the value of the city's parks.

The renaissance of the urban park system in Boston USA was brought about by the Boston GreenSpace Alliance, a coalition of interests from community groups and public agencies. The Alliance adopted a strong social orientation. *'There was a feeling that if the Alliance were merely a city beautiful movement or if its focus were only on traditional environmental issues or on the major downtown parks that the organisation would neither be effective nor politically viable in Boston.'* The Alliance became a significant coalition which involved journalists and it developed a sophisticated strategy for putting pressure on the Mayor and the city authorities. The Alliance attracted the interest of powerful foundations and city businesses who in turn invested money into the re–development of city parks. [47]

THE BOSTON GREENSPACE ALLIANCE

Draft indicators for measuring local sustainability were produced by the Local Government Management Board in July 1994. Although there is limited direct reference to public parks, the framework set by these indicators has important implications for public parks and how they might be managed in future. Several indicators refer to issues such as composting garden waste; the distribution of open land; land lost to development; the practice of organic gardening methods; changes in areas of natural habitats; percentage of allotments in use; number of child care spaces available; percentage of overweight children; availability of recycling facilities; community participation in environmental improvement schemes; membership of local voluntary groups; percentage of car-free areas; and trees planted. Agenda 21 provides a broader framework within which parks can play a crucial role.

Indicators for success

We have learned a lot about the problems and inadequacies of current methods of **consultation**. There is a dire need for more sophisticated, open minded and responsive methods of involving people in decision making. As well as consultation some have high hopes that the adoption of Agenda 21 thinking can also precipitate more flexible, less bureaucratic and much more **radical approaches to funding** community groups and activities. The indicators have to **make sense** to individuals and community groups so that they can take part in measuring them.

Challenges to local authorities

Recent research carried out for Lancashire County Council points to the unfamiliarity of the term 'sustainability' amongst the public at large and the seemingly impersonal nature of 'sustainability' themes with their distance from everyday concerns about money, jobs, or questions of health. [48] In our view, urban parks have many qualities which suggest that they should be at the heart of local strategies, and they provide a good starting point from which to explore three areas that are proving crucial to the development of Agenda 21. Firstly, parks are obvious public places in which to try out and demonstrate certain practical applications of 'sustainability' in urban localities. Secondly, the emphasis of our study has been on the social value of parks, and park use provides a practical way of approaching the social issues Agenda 21 seeks to embrace, such as children's freedom and mobility, fitness and health, and access to public places. Thirdly, an openness and willingness to try out new kinds of public participation in the management of parks can provide more genuine and more sophisticated methods of consulting, involving and listening to people's ideas.

Current work There are a number of recent initiatives in this field which are of direct concern to this report.

- The Local Government Management Board (LGMB) have brought out a range of information booklets to assist local authorities in getting to grips with LA21. They have also sponsored the Sustainable Indicators project.

- United Nations Association through its close links with UNED-UK, was one of the first organisations to offer help to local authorities and through its Sustainable Communities Project is working directly with six local authorities on pilot projects.

- The World Wildlife Fund (WWF) is currently seeking LA21 partnerships with up to 20 local authorities and has already embarked on a community led LA21 project with Reading Borough Council.

- The Wildlife Trusts through their Environment City initiative are working with Leicester and Peterborough, whilst some individual county wildlife trusts are building on existing community links to develop initiatives at the parish and district level.

- In London the London Ecology Centre has established a Local Agenda 21 Network. The London Ecology Unit is also active in the area.

- The Government itself has established its 'Going for Green' initiative, one of the objectives of which is to establish four pilot 'sustainable communities' to test and report on the relevance and practicability of sustainable lifestyles.

Future work Among the issues which might be examined in greater depth, the evidence of this report suggests the need for a clearer understanding of the following trends:

- The extent of increasing social polarisation in towns and cities: jobs, housing, educational and leisure opportunities;

- The breaking of spatial linkages between work, home, education and leisure; zoning, impact of out–of–town retailing; dormitory suburbs and marginalised public housing estates without work or social facilities;

- Current urban transport issues; decline of public transport; social relationships and attitudes around cars, bicycles and pedestrians;

- Estimated strength of the voluntary sector, and mutual aid schemes;

- Alternative economies, LETS schemes, and 'new economics' thinking about labour exchange schemes;

- Organisational capacity of local government to effect change and encourage the culture of consultation;

- The factors which exclude people from the free and unhindered use of public space;

- The 24 hour city and the night–time economy; can urban consolidation in both time and space, prevent the further process of counter–urbanisation, and the resulting wastefulness of resources?

In all of these issues, parks have a central role to play.

The Victorians had only one model for the urban park—today there are many, if we could only understand them and recognise the range and diversity. Rather than trying to squeeze them into existing management, funding and maintenance regimes, local authorities should welcome this new diversity and respond generously to these new opportunities. We envisage in future a much more varied portfolio, with local authorities directly managing some parks and open spaces, while other are managed in partnership with community groups, ecology groups, and other organisations such as schools, hospitals, even businesses. Some indeed are already beginning to do this. In this model a well thought out grants programme has to be taken seriously, for it could release a lot of energy and commitment among local people. It should be noted that many community gardens, farms and wildlife trusts were originally financed by the more flexible grant opportunities available through Urban Aid and the Community Programme. Flexible grants programmes are vital to local vitality. In this model the park can re–establish itself at the heart of local development across a wide range of issues—health, ecology, community development, urban design and planning—which are the pre–conditions for a better quality of life in the future.

The extended family

Section VIII WAYS FORWARD:
THINKING ABOUT THE MECHANISMS FOR
CHANGE—AND SOME RECOMMENDATIONS

Many of the problems now faced by urban parks stem from the way that they have been *taken for granted*. Partly—but not only—as a result of continuing central government constraints on local government spending, their management has been largely restricted to basic maintenance, and local authorities have little information about the way they are used. Parks managers have been effectively demoted within local authority hierarchies, and the interest in parks has often been superseded by an interest in newer forms of leisure provision. Responsibility for parks has often been buried within a sub–section of a department or directorate, and the connections between parks and the wider public realm, leisure provision, the ecology of the city, private leisure trends, questions of health, (both physical and mental) and of urban safety have not been made. Funding for public parks has also been reduced as local authorities have struggled to balance their budgets in a context of ever diminishing financial resources.

The ways parks have been managed have not responded to the changing patterns of people's lives, nor to the changing structure of cities and to urban policy concerns with the ways people now live in cities. Few local authorities have found ways of introducing innovation, new activities and facilities, or ways of allowing individuals and groups a role in the running and management of urban parks. New sources of funding have also been difficult to identify and garner.

The problems of parks are entrenched in these questions of management. Many local authorities have begun to get to grips with these issues by working out strategies, introducing new professional skills and by allowing and encouraging other groups and organisations to take part in the provision of parks. The following section outlines a way forward for urban parks by re–integrating them with wider conceptions of the role of public space in cities.

MANAGEMENT PLANS AND BUDGETS

There is no general new model ready to be applied to all parks. The starting point is to understand the distinctive qualities of each park and its locality. The most recent local parks strategies have recognised the need to prepare a strategy that establishes the differences between parks and the specific management requirements of each one. This approach does away with the notion that all parks are the same, and that all that is required is a blanket maintenance programme funded by a single rolling budget. Instead money spent on each park should be tied to a tailor–made management plan for each individual park. This would involve, as a minimum:

1. Defining the purpose of each park and open space;

2. Undertaking at least a minimal form of survey to establish who uses the space/park and what for;

3. Re–formulating budgets so that expenditure is tied to objectives;

4. Working locally and nationally to develop new planning guidelines for open space that is more flexible and responsive to local needs.

Parks Investment Funds

A number of local authorities—Bromley, Bristol and Sheffield, for example—are experimenting with ways of creating investment funds as well as maintenance funds for their local parks. This can be done by ring–fencing savings made through CCT, through strategically prioritising certain parks for additional expenditure, or a judicious policy of disposals (land sales), the monies raised being specifically tied to parks improvement programmes. The issue of selling public land is highly contentious, and each case needs to be considered on its own merits. But it has to be considered a serious option. In Sheffield, consultant Alan Barber has recommended the establishment of a Parks Investment Fund, 'with capital receipts from the disposal of not more than 10% of all open space for alternative development...The proposed Parks Investment fund is intended to kick–start the programme to revitalise the inner–city parks.' We would strongly endorse such a programme.

MANAGEMENT OF PUBLIC SPACE

Public parks should be seen as an integral part of the public realm. They are part of a continuum of public space which includes town centres, squares, pedestrianised streets, traffic–calmed residential streets, among a myriad of other kinds of open spaces. Public parks need to brought into this frame and managed accordingly. The integration of public space implies a re–conception of its management. At present responsibilities for managing public land fall, for example, onto Housing Departments (the open space within housing estates); Highways Departments (roadside areas); Planning Departments (town centre, streets, squares, canal towpaths and greenchain walks); Leisure Departments (parks, commons, and cemeteries), and so on. The detailed by–laws that pertain to each kind of public space can be quite different in each instance. Similarly, management methods and practice are very different in each place. What is now needed is a strategy for the management of public space that looks across all these different kinds of spaces and develops ways of improving the management and quality and standard of all public areas.

Integrated public space will require new forms of management. Town centre management provides one model for the positive management of public space. It would be interesting to develop the notion that at least one senior officer within each local authority be given the role of

✓ YES

YES YES ✓

over–seeing all relevant policies on the safety, accessibility and quality of local public space, and co–ordinating initiatives across all depart-ments. Such an officer would ensure that the needs of pedestrians, of those without access to cars, of those escorting children, of the elderly and the disabled were given the same kind of priority of movement and access that car drivers are given.

> Castlefields Park in central Manchester is one of the city's most successful new parks–but there isn't any grass, and there aren't any trees. It is, in fact, a conservation area at the heart of Manchester's historic industrial district, where the first canals and the first railway lines were built. It is an 'urban heritage park' and is managed as a integrated space, with a high quality of signing, interpreta-tion, educational, social and leisure facilities. It has its own park rangers who are responsible for safety and security. It is immensely successful.

The new parks ranger services currently being developed within several local authorities, whereby rangers provide educational services, lead activities and generally create a more interpretative role for parks staff, also provide a model for the management of public space. More thought needs to be given to:

RECOMMENDATIONS

> 5. Developing local strategies for improving the quality of all public space, perhaps along the lines of town centre management schemes and structures;
>
> 6. Investigating other forms of management, as appropriate to each space and local conditions: direct provision, partnership, voluntary management or Trusts and so on;
>
> 7. Developing new roles for the staffing of public space which combine a public service role, with educational, safety and maintenance role;
>
> 8. Developing a parks brief in order to work with other agencies such as social services, environmental services, and arts and leisure departments.

The new initiatives in establishing ranger services set a challenge to professional management, and the higher education establishment, to respond by providing the new education, skills and training needed for better advocacy management and future development.

AGENDA 21

Agenda 21 provides an opportunity to include urban parks within the developing framework of local consultation, community development and environmental protection. The Agenda 21 policies to date concen-trate on an environmental approach, often to the exclusion of more social objectives. Urban parks can provide a way to develop social pro-jects under the Agenda 21 banner and redress the current imbalance. Understanding the way people would like to use public parks provides a way of thinking through the role in which the public realm can contribute to the idea of sustainability.

RECOMMENDATIONS

9.   Establish an 'experimental fund' for local parks–based initiatives which demonstrate how environmental, economic and social issues interact and can be made to work together for the common good.

10.   Experiment with more radical and sophisticated forms of popular consultation on sustainability issues, which people can understand, respond to and trust.

11.   Liaise with health authorities to establish a clearer role for parks in the wider issues of public health, fitness and well–being

URBAN REGENERATION

Urban parks should be placed at the centre of DoE and local authority urban regeneration policies and funding strategies. At present central government, through the Countryside Commission, is responsible for developing policy for managing the use of the countryside. There is no equivalent remit for urban open space. In the light of the wide consensus on the need to consolidate urban quality of life for ecological, social and other reasons, there is a need for more strategic thinking around these issues at central government level.

RECOMMENDATIONS

12.   Where feasible they should be included within Single Regeneration Budget Bids, (including Safer Cities).

13.   Urban parks should have a high profile in the DoE urban quality initiative.

14.   The DoE should collate and distribute best practice information.

15.   A PPG on urban parks may help to set frameworks for local strategies.

LOTTERY FUNDING

Urban parks should be considered as suitable sites for investment from Lottery funds. Whether for direct investment in the parks themselves, or for buildings and facilities within them, it ought to be possible to develop bids for at least four out of the five Lottery Boards, namely: the Millennium fund, the National Heritage Memorial fund, the Arts fund and the Sports Fund. However, in order to make certain that investment in urban parks is effective and lasting the following principles may serve as basic funding guidelines. Lottery Funding should not be restricted to the re–investment in the physical fabric of the park but should be open to proposals for new buildings, events and activities in parks.

RECOMMENDATIONS

> 16. Investment should be a part of a wider local strategy for urban parks
>
> 17. The park/s selected for investment should exhibit signs of potential success. Ideally the park/s should be in a mixed residential area, it should be reasonably accessible and have a mix of activities.
>
> 18. The application should demonstrate the ways in which people of all ages will find elements of interest in the park.
>
> 19. The application should demonstrate the ways in which local groups and individuals can be involved in the care and management of the park.
>
> 20. The proposal should indicate ways in which the sense of safety in the park will be enhanced. (Mobile patrols alone are not sufficient.)

how?

START WITH THE PARK!

In many 'developed' societies, economists and politicians are increasingly puzzled by the fact that increased material wealth no longer automatically produces an increased sense of well–being. The 'feel–good' factor has gone missing from the traditional equation that prosperity equals happiness. For with wealth, particularly so when it is unevenly distributed, come envy, crime, stress, pollution and insecurity. In the search for new values, based less on material wealth and more on the quality of personal and social relationships and community, together with a restored relationship to the natural world, the urban park could once again come into its own as a site for social renewal. There is an echo here of the sentiments that inspired the new town movement in Britain after the war. Asked what was the foundation stone of these new communities, one of the founding architect–planners, Don Ritson, simply stated that one should *'Start with the park!'*

NOTES

1   The Dublin case study was undertaken in association with the Nexus research
    agency for a consortium of Dublin local authorities which were keen to share
    findings.

2   Raymond Williams's *The Country and the City*, is a discussion of the changes in
    social and literary perceptions of the nature of country and city and the
    relationship between them. Paladin 1975.

3   Karasov, Deborah, in *The Once & Future Park*, Princeton University Press, 1993

4   Dunk, Julie & Rugg, Julie, T*he Management of Old Cemetery Land*, Shaw & Sons,
    1994

5   Philip Kivell, *Land and City*, patterns and processes of urban change. Routledge,
    London 1993. Page xii.

6   William Solesbury, 'Spatial Issues: New Times, New Places, New Strategies' in
    Managing the Metropolis: Metroplitan Renaissance: New Life For Old City Regions. ed.
    Roberts, Peter et al. (Aldershot England Avebury 1993)

7   DoE *Urban Land Markets in the United Kingdom.* HMSO 1988

8   *Urbanisation and the Function of Cities* in the European Community. Commission
    of the European Communities, Brussels, Luxembourg 1992. European Institute
    for Urban Affairs, Liverpool John Moores University.

9   Philip Kivell, *Land and City, patterns and processes of urban change.* Routledge,
    London 1993. (page 88)

10 *Household change in the 1980s: a review*, Michael Murphy and Ann Berrington,
    Department of Population Studies, London School of Economics. Population
    Trends No 73 Autumn 1993. HMSO

8   *Spatial variations in ethnic minority group populations in Great Britain.* David Owen,
    Centre for Research in Ethnic Relations, University of Warwick. Population
    Trends No.78 Winter 1994.

12 Hillman, Mayer, *Children, Transport and the Quality of Life,* Policy Studies Institute,
    1993

13 Jan Oosterman, *Cafe Culture, Urban Space and the Public Realm, in The 24 Hour
    City: Selected Papers from the First National Conference on the Night–time Economy,*
    Edited by Andrew Lovatt, Manchester Metropolitan University, Institute for
    Popular Culture 1994. (page 122).

14 *Viability and Vitality in Town Centres.* URBED. HMSO 1994.

15 See Richard Rogers & Mark Fisher *A New London*, Penguin Books 1992, and
    Richard Rogers Reith Lectures February 1995.

16 Richard Rogers, 1st Reith Lecture delivered on the 12th February 1995.

17 Lyn Lofland, discussed in *People in cities: the urban environment and its effects.*
    Edward Krupat. Cambridge University Press 1985.

18 Jacquie Burgess, *The Politics of Trust.* Parks Working Paper No. 8 Comedia 1994.

19 *City Sense and City Design. Writings and Projects of Kevin Lynch*, ed. T. Bannerjee
    and M. Southworth. MIT Press 1990.

20 Hilary Taylor Working Paper No 10, *Age and Order: The park as a metaphor for a
    civilized society.* Comedia and Demos Working Papers. 1994.

21 *City Sense and City Design. Writings and Projects of Kevin Lynch*, ed. T. Bannerjee
    and M. Southworth. MIT Press 1990

22 Massey, Doreen, *Space, Place & Gender,* Polity Press, 1994

23 Margaret Crawford, *The world in a shopping mall, in Variations on a Theme Park.*
    Ed Michael Sorkin, Noonday Press 1992. New York.

24   Ralf Ebert, *Modern Parks in Germany*, Comedia Working Paper No. 12. Comedia 1995.

25   Tom Turner, *Open Space Planning in London*. TPR, 63 (4) 1992

26   See Horticulture Week, No 19, June 16th 1994.

27   Davis, Mike, *Beyond Blade Runner: Urban Control & The Ecology of Fear*, USA 1994

28   *Urban Parks: A Discussion Paper from the Landscape Institute*, 1992, p8

29   Cited in *The Once and Future Park*, op.cit.

30   Kent, Bruce, Report for the Haringey Leisure Sub–Committee, 27/9/94

31   Bob Hughes, *Lost Childhoods: The case for children's play*, Comedia & Demos The Future of Public Parks Working Paper No. 3, March 1994.

32   Wendy Titman, *Special Places, Special People: the hidden curriculum of school grounds*. WWF/Learning through Landscapes. 1994.

33   Bromley Parks and Spaces, Research Report RAS Ltd, London 1994.

34   Welch, David, *Management of Urban Parks*, Longman 1991

35   *Watch this Space!*, London Boroughs Association, 1995, p34

36   Dunk, Julie & Rugg, Julie, Op cit.

37   Quoted in the article by Bill Swan, *Horticulture Week*, 19th January 1995

38   Wright, Patrick, *A Journey Through Ruins*, 1991

39   *Assessing the Impact of Urban Policy. Inner Cities Research Programme*, Universities of Manchester, Liverpool and Durham. HMSO 1994.

40   *City and Town Life*, (Editorial) The Lancet, 28/5/94, p1303 (2)

41   *Allied Dunbar National Fitness Survey. Summary Paper*, The Sports Council & Health Education Council 1992.

42   Michael Collins *The Sporting Life: Sport, Health & Recreation in Urban Parks*. Working Paper No. 11. Comedia & Demos 1994.

43   English Nature Report No 22, *Human Well–being, natural landscapes and wildlife in rural areas*, C.L.E. Rhode & A.D. Kendle. Reading University 1994. See also The Biophilia Hypothesis, S. Kellert & E. Wilson, Island Press 1993.

44   *The Peckham Experiment, a study of the living structure of society*. Innes Pearce, Lucy Crocker. Allen Unwin. 1943.

45   *Reality & Perception*, G. Godbey, National Recreation and Parks Association, January 1993.

46   From a report by Charles Landry, Comedia.

47   Primack Mark, *Renaissance of an Urban Park System: The Boston Story*. A Paper prepared for the Rene Dubos Only One Earth Forum.

48   *Public Perceptions and sustainability in Lancashire: Indicators, Institutions, Participation. A report by the Centre for the Study of Environmental Change*, commissioned by Lancashire County Council. March 1995.

BIBLIOGRAPHY

Adams, William Howard — *Nature Perfected*, Abbeville Press, 1991

Audit Commission — *Competitive Management of Parks and Green Spaces*, HMSO, London 1988

Bell, Sandra — *Watch This Space!*, An LBA Report, London Boroughs Association, 1995

Bedford Borough Council — *Bedford Parks and Green Space: A Position Statement*, 1993

Burgess, Jacquelin, Harrison, Carolyn and Limb, Melanie — *People, parks and the urban green: a study of popular meanings and values for open spaces in the City*, in Urban Studies (25), pp 455–473. 1988

Burgess, Jacquelin, Harrison, Carolyn — *Nature in the city–popular values for a living world*, Journal of Environment Management, Vol 25 (1987)

Burton, N., — *Urban Parks Wardening*, ILAM, 1993

Centre for the Study of Environmental Change, Lancaster University — *Leisure Landscapes, Leisure, Culture and the English Countryside: Challenges and Conflicts*. CPRE 1994

Centre for Leisure & Tourism Studies, University of North London — *Royal Parks Surveys*, 1994

Chadwick, George F. — *The Park and the Town, Public Landscape in the 19th & 20th centuries*, Architectural Press, 1966

Clouston, Brian — 'Urban Parks in Crisis', Landscape Design, June 1984

Conway, Hazel — *People's parks: the design and development of Victorian parks in Britain*, Cambridge University Press, 1991

Cranz, Galen — *The Politics of Park Design, A History of Urban Parks in America*, MIT Press, 1989

Cranz, Galen — *Women in urban parks, in SIGNS: Journal of Women in Culture and Society* (5)3 suppl., pp 579–595. 1980

Crouch, D., & Ward, C. — *The Allotment: its Landscape and Culture*, Faber & Faber 1988

Countryside Commission — *Quality of Countryside: Quality of Life, the Countryside Commission's prospectus into the next century*, Countryside Commission 1995

Department of Environment — *Quality in Town and Country* HMSO 1994

Department of Environment — *Sustainable Development: The UK Strategy*, HMSO 1994

Department of Environment — *Trees in Towns*, HMSO 1993

Dunk, Julie & Rugg, Julie — *The Management of Old Cemetery Land*, Shaw & Sons, 1994

DoE, Inner Cities Directorate   *Greening City Sites*, HMSO 1987

Fisher, A., & Gerster, G.,   *The Art of the Maze*, Wiedenfield & Nicholson,
                                       1990

Fletcher, John   *Time to pay up at the park?*, Horticulture Week,
                                       vol 215, No 7, 17 February 1994

Harrison, Robert Pogue   *Forests: The Shadow of Civilization*, University of
                                       Chicago Press, 1992

Harvey, David   *Social Justice and the City*, London 1973

Hillman, Mayer (ed.)   *Children, Transport & the Quality of Life*, PSI, 1993

ILAM   *A Guide to Management Plans for Parks & Open
                                       Spaces*, ILAM 1991

The Garden History Society   *Public Prospects, Historic Urban Parks under
& The Victorian Society   Threat*, 1993

GMB   *Grounds for Concern*, 1993

Greed, H., Clara   *Women and Planning: creating gendered realities*,
                                       Routledge, 1994

Green, N.,   *The Spectacle of Nature*, Manchester University
                                       Press, 1990

Karasov, Deborah   *The Once and Future Park*, Princeton Arch-
& Waryan, Steve   itectural Press, 1993

Kern, Stephen   *The Culture of Time and Space 1880–1918*,
                                       Harvard University Press, 1983

Kivell, Philip   *Land and City, Patterns and processes of urban
                                       change*, Routledge, 1993

Landry, C., & Bianchini, F.,   *The Creative City*, Demos/Comedia, 1995

Lasdun, Susan   *The English Park*, Andre Deutsch, 1991

Llewelyn–Davies,   *Planning & Environmental Trust Associates Ltd
                                       Open Space Planning in London*, LPAC, 1992

Lynch, Kevin   *City Sense and City Design, The Writings and
                                       Projects of Kevin Lynch*, edited by T. Bannerjee
                                       and M. Southworth, MIT Press, 1990

Massey, Doreen   *Space, Place and Gender*, Polity Press, 1994

Morphet, Janice   *Provision and Protection of Open Space*, in
                                       Leisure Manager 1991

Morphet, Janice   *Urban Open Space–from Space to Place*, in The
                                       Planner/TCPSS Proceedings, 14th December
                                       1990

Murray, Ian & Ford, Richard   *Wandsworth Tories want to form their own police
                                       force*, The Times, 24/8/94

Herbert Muschamp et al   *The Once and Future Park*, Princeton
                                       Architectural Press, 1993.

Nicholson–Lord, David   *The Greening of the Cities*, RKP 1987

Planning Exchange   *International City Parks and Civic Spaces Project.
                                       Phase 1: Review of Strategy, investment and
                                       management practices.* A report to Glasgow
                                       development Agency, August 1993

Pleydell–Bouverie, Jaspar   *Before its time: sustainable buildings*, The
                                       Guardian, 7/1/95

Plummer, B., & Shewan, D.,	*City Gardens: An Open Spaces Survey in the City of London*, Corporation of London, Belhaven Press, 1992
Popper, Sir Karl	This quotation is taken from the catalogue to *The Ulster Saga, paintings by Gerry Gleason*, Middlesbrough Art Gallery, 1995
Poulsen, Charles	*Victoria Park*, Stepney Books & The Journeyman Press, 1976
Rhode, C.L.E. & Kendle, A.D.	*Human well-being, Natural Landscapes and Wildlife in Urban Areas, A Review.* English Nature 1994
Robson, et al	*Assessing The Impact of Urban Policy,* DoE Inner Cities Research Programme. HMSO 1994
Sorkin, Michael	*Variations on a Theme Park, the New American City and the End of Public Space*, The Noonday Press, New York, 1992
Streetwise	Quarterly Bulletin of the National association for Urban Studies (ongoing)
Swan, Bill	*For Better or for Worse, The CCT Survey*, Horticulture Week, 19/1/95
Tate, Alan & Turner, Tom	*Urban Parks—Discussion Paper*, Landscape Institute, 1993
Titman, Wendy	*Special places, special people: the hidden curriculum of school grounds*, WWF/ Learning through landscapes, 1994
Topos	European Landscape Magazine, Urban Open Space, 5th December 1993
Turner, Tom	*Towards a Green Strategy For London*, LPAC, 1991
Walmsley, DJ	*Urban Living*, Longman 1988
Ward, Colin	*The Child in the City* Bedford Square Press, 1990
Ward, Colin	*Welcome Thinner City*, Bedford Square Press, 1989
Welch, David	*Management of Urban Parks*, Longman, 1991
Whyte, William, H.,	*City, Rediscovering the Centre*, Anchor Books, Doubleday, New York, 1988
Women's Design Service	*It's Not all Swings and Roundabouts: making better play space for the under-sevens*, London, undated.
Worpole, Ken	*Towns for People*, Open University Press, 1993
Wright, Patrick	*A Journey Through Ruins*, Paladin 1992
Zukin, Sharon	*Landscapes of Power*, University of California Press, 1991

Appendix 1 THE COMEDIA QUANTITATIVE RESEARCH

This Appendix describes in detail the findings of the observation exercises, interviews and the household surveys carried out as part of the case–study work. The observation exercises were carried out in eight different parks and the interviews were held in ten parks. The household surveys were carried out in Southwark and in Cardiff. Overall, 10,250 people were observed, 1,211 people interviewed and 295 household questionnaires were returned.

The research was primarily carried out to meet individual case–study objectives. In most instances the same observation sheets were used and the procedures for observation followed a common format. The parks were observed for 12 hour periods, from 8am to 8pm. Similarly, the same questionnaire was used in interview surveys.

The results from the observation, interviews and household surveys show a high degree of consistency. Similar patterns of park use were found in most of the 10 parks. In the absence of national data on park use the findings from these surveys provide a significant first step in showing how urban parks in Britain are used.

THE OBSERVATION EXERCISE

For the purposes of the study, an observation exercise and survey form was devised to administer in parks, briefly noting down the characteristics of all people entering a particular park on a particular day. Observers were positioned to cover all entrances and exits. The form was designed to note park users according to:

- gender
- entering the park with or without a baby in a pushchair (hence age and sex indeterminate)
- entering a park with a dog or dogs
- approximate age group,
- alone or with others
- ethnicity (White/Afro–Caribbean/Asian)
- physical disability.

In all, 10,250 people were observed during the summer of 1994, mostly on Sundays, and in eight different parks, some of which were surveyed on more than one occasion. The parks were: Poulter Park (LB Sutton), Albert Park (Middlesbrough), Inwood Park (LB Hounslow), Maryon Park (LB Greenwich), Victoria Park (Cardiff), Brunswick Gardens (LB Southwark), St Andrew's Park (Bristol) and Charlton Park (LB Greenwich). In all cases the park observation exercise was a constituent feature of the local case study. It was also often the first occasion for a long time when actual numbers of users had been counted. Lampton Park and Heston Park in Hounslow, and Abbey Park in Leicester were also observed, and counts taken, albeit with slightly different questionnaires and methodology.

This 'broad brush' survey, the first of its kind as far as we know in the UK, should be treated with some caution obviously. It took place during one of the hottest summers on record, and almost always on Sunday. Seasonal and weekday variations are likely to be significant. Yet its findings are complemented by the questionnaire administered, which sought to monitor and record more general patterns of use.

Of the 10,250 park users observed, 6114 were male and 4,136 female, **Gender** giving an average ratio across all age groups of male users to women users of 60%: 40%. There were some significant variations on this, park by park. The highest percentage of female park users (47%) was recorded at Maryon Park, Greenwich, on Sunday 3rd July 1994, and lowest percentage of female park users (33%) was recorded in Poulter Park, Sutton on Sunday 24th July, 1994. But in general the 6:4 ratio was reflected almost uniformly across all parks.

A separate record was kept of very young babies either carried into the **Babies & buggies** park or pushed in a pram or buggy. This was a fairly infrequent occurrence, making up as little as 1% of the total count, and never more than 5%.

The presence of dogs in parks remains one of the most contentious is- **Dogs** sues in current park management and public concern. Again this survey may be one of the first to quantify the issue. Averaged out across all the parks surveyed, the ratio of dogs to humans was 1: 8.5. Here there were quite large local variations, with the highest ratio of dogs to humans recorded in Poulter Park, Sutton on Sunday 31st July 1994, of 1:4, and the lowest ratio of 1:16 recorded in both Maryon Park, Greenwich on 3rd July 1994 and in Albert Park, Middlesbrough on Sunday, August 21st, 1994. It was also observed that people bring dogs into parks generally either early in the morning or last thing at night: there are clear time–determined patterns of dog use.

Because people were categorised by age according to subjective deci- **Age Groups** sions made by observers, too much should not be read into these patterns and figures. The broad age categories used were: Toddlers, Children, Teenagers, Young Adults, Middle Aged & Elderly. Broadly speaking Toddlers, Children and Teenagers made up between 30%–40% of park users, and Young Adults, Middle Aged and Elderly between 60% and 70% of all park users. Between them, two age categories—Young Adults and Middle Aged—made up more than 50% of all park users. There may be two areas of surprise or concern which would warrant further investigation—the significant use made of parks by teenagers and young adults (often perceived as 'anti–social' age groups), and the significant under–representation of the elderly in this survey of actual park users: as little as 5% in Maryon Park (3/7/94) and never more than 20% (weekday, Cardiff, but only 11% in the same park on a Sunday). A separate section has been written on Teenage Use of Parks.

Alone or with others Approximately one third of people observed entering parks came on their own, one third came with one other person, and a final third of park users came as part of a larger group. Whether these patterns are connected with perceptions of safety or gregariousness, the fact is that parks are seen and used as a place to visit with other people. Even the people who came alone were often those accompanied by dogs. Women on their own was a sight sufficiently unusual to warrant particular comment by observers on the observation sheets.

For example, of the 559 people who were observed to use Poulter Park on Sunday, 24th July 1994, 376 were male (67%) and 183 were female (33%). Of those 183 females, only 6 came completely unaccompanied, whilst another 27 came 'alone', but with a dog. Another two women came 'alone', with a baby buggy. Women on their own in public places such as parks remain a rare phenomenon, and from observation are likely to be teenage girls who have pre–arranged to meet friends at an agreed location. Yet it also has to be said that solitary men also represent a minority of park users.

Ethnicity Ethnicity is also connected with group use. In general it was found that ethnic minority use of parks quite closely followed local demographic patterns of ethnic minority representation in the local population. For example, in Albert Park, Middlesbrough, 9% of those recorded entering the park were deemed to have been of Asian origin, whereas 25% of those entering Inwood Park, Hounslow were deemed to have been of Asian origin; both figures reflect quite closely the ethnic minority make up of the local populations. The 21% Afro–Caribbean use of Maryon Park, Greenwich and the 31% Afro–Caribbean use of Brunswick Gardens, Southwark, again closely reflects local demographics. In short, parks appear to be well used by ethnic minority groups.

However ethnic minority use is more patterned and time–governed. When the ethnicity breakdown was correlated with time of day, the results of the Maryon Park survey showed that 'non–white' presence in the park peaked in the afternoon and for a brief period of less than an hour black and Asian family groups exceeded the numbers of white park users.

In the Middlesbrough survey, the most distinctive patterns of ethnic minority use emerged, in terms of entrances, time of day and weekday/weekend differentials. For example on a weekday morning at the Dorman entrance the majority of users (98%) were 'White' with

'Asian' users amounting to only 1%. In total contrast the survey conducted at the Clairville entrance on the 4pm–8pm shift on a weekday produced 72% 'White', 26% 'Asian', 2% 'Afro–Caribbean'. To generalise, Asian users came to the park in groups, in the early evening and at weekends, mostly through one particular entrance. This pattern has also emerged in the Leicester and Hounslow surveys where there are also significant Asian populations: Asian use is family–based or group–based, and occurs mostly during the early evening and at weekends, particularly on Sunday afternoons.

The observation exercise was designed to record the presence of people with evident physical disabilities, but such users never amounted to more than 0.5% of all users, and again this is an area of park use that requires further investigation, given that, disabled people form 10% of the population.

Disabled people

INTERVIEWS WITH PARK USERS

In conjunction with the observation exercise, short interviews were carried out with park users. The questionnaire was designed to elicit basic information about the way people used the parks. The interviewers asked how and how far people had travelled to the park, how frequently they visited the park and how long they anticipated staying in the park. The questionnaire also asked people about their use of the countryside and whether they had their own, or access to a private garden. Park users were also asked whether concerns about their safety had ever deterred then from using the park. The interviews also included two open ended questions to allow people to make further comments about the park and to make suggestions for its improvement.

In all, 1,211 people were interviewed on 10 separate dates in 10 different parks. Very broadly this figure represents more than 10% (11.8%) of the number of people observed using the parks. The parks where interviews took place were:

COMEDIA'S 1994
PARK SURVEYS

Inwood Park, Hounslow	29th May
Abbey Park, Leicester	29th June (Weds)
Maryon Park, Greenwich	3rd July
Abbey Park, Leicester	10th July
Lampton Park, Hounslow	7th July (Thurs)
Heston Park, Hounslow	12th July (Tues)
Heston Park, Hounslow	16th July (Sat)
Inwood Park, Hounslow	16th July (Sat)
Lampton Park, Hounslow	23rd July (Sat)
Poulter Park, Sutton	24th July
Inwood Park, Hounslow	26th July (Tues)
Poulter Park, Sutton	31st July
Heeley City Farm, Sheffield	7th August
St Andrews, Bristol	7th August
Charlton Park, Greenwich	21st August
Victoria Park, Cardiff	4th September
Brunswick Park, Southwark	11th September

The following analysis draws together all the park surveys and presents comparative findings from the 10 parks in which surveys were carried out during the summer of 1994.

Travel time The results from all the surveys show that the majority of park users interviewed live close to the parks they use. By far the great majority of park users took less than five minutes to get to their park. More than 90% of park users interviewed in all the surveys took less than 15 minutes to reach the park. Taking an average across all the parks 68% of users said it took them less than five minutes to get to the park.

Means of travel People walk to parks. Strikingly, the figures from all the surveys show that more than 69% of all those interviewed in every park walked to the park. 69% was the lowest % recorded (in Sutton). All the other park surveys showed percentages of 77% or more for walking as the means of getting to the park. 93% of those surveyed in Brunswick Park in Southwark had walked to the park; 84% of interviewees in Maryon Park in Greenwich had walked to the park. Cars were used typically by 12% of park users. All the surveys showed very similar pattern of car use. The highest level of car use was found in Inwood park in Hounslow, with people parking in the residential streets around the park. The presence or not of a car park in the park does not seem to have much of a bearing on the % of people travelling by car, (although the ease with which people can park in the surrounding streets may be a factor). Organised sports, football and rugby matches and a good children's playground appear to attract car borne visitors. Bicycles were used by fewer than 5% of park users interviewed in these surveys, and travel by bus accounted for less than 5% of visitors interviewed. Walking and driving are the two most significant means of travelling to local parks.

Park users tend to visit their local park very frequently. In every survey but one, more than 40% of people interviewed said they visited the park daily. (It should be noted that dog–walking accounts for a lot of people using parks on a daily basis.) The findings are very consistent across all the parks. The highest figures are found in Hounslow, where 63% of people interviewed in Heston park said they visited daily, and Bristol and Cardiff where 48% of people interviewed in each of the parks said they visited the park every day. The lowest figure was found in Charlton in Greenwich where 37% of people interviewed said they visited every day. The figures for twice weekly use also appear to be relatively consistent across all the parks. The surveys show that the average for twice weekly visits is 24% of respondents. The figures for weekly visits ranged from 11% in Southwark to 24% in Sutton. The low weekly use for Southwark reflects the higher daily use, as the park is commonly used as a pedestrian short cut. The higher figure for Sutton may reflect the numbers of people involved in weekly sports matches. All the surveys show that people visiting the parks once a month accounts for 10% or less of those interviewed.

Frequency of use

Together the surveys reveal a consistent pattern of use. An average across all the parks shows that 45% of people surveyed used the parks every day, 23% is the average for twice weekly, the weekly average drops to 17%, while the average for monthly visits drops still further to 7%.

The findings show that 50% or more of those interviewed across all the parks planned to stay for up to 30 minutes. A significant minority ranging from 20–30% across all the parks intended to stay up to an hour in the park. The average for those intending to stay more than an hour is 20%. Clearly, time spent in the park is dependent upon variable factors such as the weather conditions. Nevertheless, there does appear to be a discernible pattern which suggests that the majority of visitors stay for short periods but significant minorities (20–30%) stay for an hour or more in the parks.

Time spent in the park

Perhaps unsurprisingly (since these people were in the parks) people interviewed did not generally feel unsafe in the park during the day. In most instances more than 70% of people said that they had not been deterred from using the park. However, people often qualified their response either by expressing concern for the safety of others, for example, fears for their children's safety, or they made it clear that their feelings of security only applied to the hours of daylight. Many people remarked on the fact that they would not consider using the parks in the evening.

Feelings about safety

The highest percentages for those that said they had been deterred from using the park because of fears for their personal safety were in Southwark where 34% of those interviewed said they had been put off using the park. In most other parks the percentages range from 16% to

26% of respondents who had been worried about using the park. These figures suggest that the majority of park users are not too fearful about their safety, but it is worth remembering that these are people already in the parks. In this light, the possibility that between 16%– 26% of those already in the parks are, or have been, concerned about their safety appears more significant.

Reasons for visiting the park

Defining why people visit parks is notoriously difficult. People may have many reasons, some may be to do with the attractions of the park, others may be more to do with getting out, getting away or finding a place to talk. Nevertheless, taking children to parks does seem to be an important factor behind many park visits. The questionnaire asked people to state their main purpose or reason for visiting the park. The response 'accompanying a child' was the single most important reason for people interviewed in St Andrews, Bristol, Victoria Park, Cardiff and Inwood Park and Heston park in Hounslow. Inwood Park has a good children's playground for a park of its size and this clearly provides an attraction within the park. Animals are also a strong attraction. 82% of visitors surveyed at Heeley City Farm in Sheffield said they came to bring children.

Taking dogs for walks is also a clear reason for park use. Although there is some variation from park to park. Some parks seem to be used more heavily by dog walkers than others. Poulter park in Sutton had high numbers of dog walkers whereas Maryon Park in Greenwich had far fewer people referring to dogs as their reason for using the park.

Visiting the countryside

The majority of people in all the surveys said they visited the countryside outside their towns or cities once a month or a few times a year. The numbers of people who said they never visited the countryside were significant, particularly those people living in London. 43% of those interviewed in Southwark said they never visited. In Greenwich the figures were 34% & 39% on two different occasions.

Access to a garden

Apart from the surveys in Maryon park in Greenwich and Brunswick park in Southwark, all the other surveys show that the majority of people had access to a private garden. More than 78% of all those interviewed had their own or shared a private garden. In Cardiff, 90% of people interviewed had a garden, in Sutton 83% of those interviewed had a garden, in the Hounslow parks 72% and 78% of people had their own gardens. In contrast, 56% of park users in Maryon park, and 48% in Brunswick park did not have their own gardens.

Access to a car

The survey results suggest that car ownership is generally lower than garden ownership. An average of 54% of people across all the surveys had access to a car. The surveys in Sutton, Hounslow and Cardiff showed the highest levels of car ownership. (The Bristol survey excluded the question on car ownership.) Again the figures for Maryon Park in Greenwich and Brunswick park in Southwark show the lowest levels of car ownership. 70% of those interviewed in Southwark and 56% of people interviewed in Maryon park did not have access to a car.

There appears to be a correlation between low car ownership and infrequent use of the countryside. Surveys in Maryon Park and Brunswick Park show the highest percentages of people who said they never went to the countryside and the highest incidence of people who said they did not have access to car.

HOUSEHOLD SURVEYS IN CARDIFF & SOUTHWARK

Another element of the quantitative research involved two household surveys, both parts of the case studies conducted in Cardiff and Southwark. In both, approximately each of 175 households immediately adjacent to Victoria Park, Cardiff, and Sunray Gardens, Southwark, were provided with 4 copies of a questionnaire about their use of their local park, which were collected a week later.

Victoria Park, Cardiff is a 20 acre 'town park' in a mixed residential area of Cardiff, well maintained, and with tennis courts, bowling green, paddling pool, children's play area, toilet block and other traditional park amenities. Sunray Gardens is a small, ornamental gardens, again in a mixed residential area, in which the main—and very attractive—feature is an ornamental pond with weeping willows, as well as tennis courts and children's play area.

Interestingly both parks serve areas which combine medium to expensive private housing with some rented local authority and private housing, and are therefore areas which have a mixture of social classes using local facilities.

The majority of the questionnaires were completed by women (Cardiff 63%, Southwark 61%), and the majority of responses came from the 25–45 age group. In Cardiff some 134 completed questionnaires were returned, and in Southwark 161 (approximately 20% of questionnaires distributed but representing nearly 50% of households returning at least one), a high response rate which suggests something of the value and interest that local people place in parks issues.

Completion Rate

34% of Cardiff people and 35% of Southwark respondents stated that they had visited the park that day, and an additional 32% of Cardiff people and 41% of Southwark respondents said that they had visited the named park within the past 7 days. Only 3% of Cardiff people and 2% of Southwark respondents claimed never to have used their local park. With, therefore, 66% of the Cardiff sample and 76% of the Southwark sample in an admittedly self–selecting but still sizeable group of local residents stating that they had visited Victoria Park or Sunray Gardens within the past week, one can only conclude that these small surveys demonstrate a very high degree of use and loyalty.

Frequency of Use

REASONS FOR USE

The main reasons people gave for visiting

	Cardiff	Southwark
To go for a walk	32%	29%
To accompany a child	21%	27%
Taking a short cut	17%	15%
To play	12.5%	14%

Only 10% of Cardiff respondents and 5% of Southwark respondents gave exercising a dog as a reason, though this is clearly a major reason which many people will not admit to.

Likes and Dislikes   Because the two parks are very different, what people most liked about each park varied, namely in Cardiff the most popular element of the park were the 'Flowers/Trees' (27%) but in Southwark it was the 'Pond' (23%). Play areas also scored high in people's responses to a choice of favourite features. The things people disliked were much more diverse, although one factor—dog excrement—was mentioned by 38% of Cardiff and 27% of Southwark respondents, by far the highest single cause of concern.

Questions of Safety   Questions of safety produced some very interesting results. The majority of respondents (92% Cardiff and 86% Southwark) claimed to feel safe in the park in daylight hours, with only 4% Cardiff and 9% Southwark claiming not to feel safe (and 5% in both surveys making no comment). Yet as a percentage, slightly more males than females claimed to feel unsafe in the park during daylight hours in both samples. In the Cardiff survey only 1 female respondent from a total of 85 female respondents stated she felt unsafe in the park. Also surprising was the fact that none of the oldest group of respondents in the Southwark sample claimed to feel unsafe during daylight hours, but within the 5–15 age group some 42% of males and 17% of females claimed to feel unsafe. Safety is often self–limiting and self–imposed. Feeling safe when you visit the park on a sunny morning is not the same as feeling safe at all times.

In many ways these figures show a degree of realism about the actual incidence of crime, for it is precisely young males who are the most common victims of crimes against the person. Yet even these small surveys indicate quite fascinating differences from the common understandings about crime and fear of crime.

Conclusions   These two surveys were carried out in two very different parks in two very different cities. Yet perhaps the dominant common factor was that each park was located in an established, mixed housing residential area. It was clear in both cases that the local park was deeply 'embedded' into the spatial and social geography of each community. This is evidenced by the high completion rate of questionnaires, and the frequency with which people claim to visit and use their local park.

The most common reasons for using these parks, people claim, are as a place to take a walk (which can also be described as an acceptable excuse to get out of the house and watch what is going on locally), or as a place to take children. People are reticent to admit that taking their dog for an exercise, as well as 'to the toilet', is a major reason for using parks, although the observation exercises clearly reveal this to be a significant reason. Both surveys showed that park users mostly claim to feel safe in their local parks during daylight hours, but among those who express some fears of safety, slightly more male than female respondents state this view.

Appendix 2 WORKING PAPERS FROM THE NATIONAL STUDY

Working Paper 1
ISBN 1 873 667 55 8

The Study Brief & Objectives. This paper outlines the distinctive approach Comedia & Demos have set themselves in their attempt to cross disciplines and boundaries to produce a new rationale for parks that will put parks back on the national and local political agenda.

Working Paper 2
ISBN 1 873 667 60 4

Law, Money & Management by Alan Barber. This paper, by one of Britain's most eminent parks specialists, looks at the history of different Acts and pieces of legislation governing the provision of parks, and at the current legislative and funding regime, nationally and locally, for parks in Britain.

Working Paper 3
ISBN 1 873 667 70 1

Lost Childhoods: Taking Children's Play Seriously, by Bob Hughes, with an introduction by Colin Ward. This paper by the editor of the International Play Journal, takes a critical look at play provision for children in Britain's towns and cities (including parks). He asks whether as a society we actually take children's needs seriously—and what problems we store up for ourselves by not doing so.

Working Paper 4
ISBN 1 873 667 75 2

Calling in the Country: Ecology, Parks and Urban Life, by David Nicholson Lord (Environmental Editor, The Independent). This paper, deliberately provocative, looks at the case for bringing nature back into the city, for the spirituality of green spaces, and for the urgent need to make cities human once again. It is the ecological argument put with great single–mindedness.

Working Paper 5
ISBN 1 873 667 26 4

Parks, Open Space and the Future of Urban Planning, by Professor Janice Morphet. This paper looks at current planning philosophies and regulations governing the provision of open space in Britain, and suggests a much more dynamic model is needed if urban green space is to be valued by communities, funded and managed properly.

Working Paper 6
ISBN 1 873 667 31 0

Lost connections and new directions: the private garden and the public park, by Martin Hoyles. This paper explores the widening gap between the world of public parks and that of the boom in private gardening. New forms of provision—gardens for the disabled, community gardens, city farms, outdoor classrooms—are urged, and existing ones identified and celebrated, if private and public realms in modern cities are not to grow even further apart.

Working Paper 7
ISBN 1 873 667 36 1

Reclaiming the Night: night–time use, lighting and safety in Britain's Parks by Carl Gardner (with Jonathan Speirs) This paper looks at the history of the night–time use of parks in Britain, arising out of the 18th & 19th century tradition of the pleasure gardens, and asks why so little attention has been paid to the effective use of lighting—both ornamental and for safety and security purposes—to make British parks 'come alive' again at night. The paper includes examples of successful lighting schemes in existing British parks. There is a detailed bibliography.

The Politics of Trust: reducing fear of crime in urban parks by Jacquie Burgess. This paper summarises and analyses current research on fear of crime in urban parks and green open spaces, particularly among women. It questions whether electronic surveillance, more mobile security patrols and other forms of anti–crime techniques in themselves will solve the larger issue of the decline of public trust. It explores the strategies by which the most vulnerable sections of the community negotiate their own safety in public spaces, and argues for new forms of mutual support and civil trust.

Working Paper 8
ISBN 1 873 667 41 8

The popular culture of city parks by David Crouch. This paper makes a strong claim for the cultural importance of the more informal, often marginal, pieces of green space and open land which are to be found in Britain's towns and cities. It criticises the recent attempt to market parks as tourist attractions at the expense of the uses and needs of local people.

Working Paper 9
ISBN 1 873 667 81 7

Age and Order: the public park as a metaphor for a civilized society by Dr Hilary A. Taylor. This paper argues that the very best of Victorian parks were designed to embody a strong moral code, involving assumptions about appropriate public behaviour and agreed attitudes towards 'nature'. Aesthetic issues were also paramount, and the Victorian park successfully absorbed Oriental influences, as well as the 'colour theories' which influenced the Impressionists and Post–Impressionists. These traditions are still relevant today.

Working Paper 10
ISBN 1 873 667 46 9

The Sporting Life: sport, health and active recreation in urban parks, by Michael F. Collins. This paper provides comprehensive and up to date facts and figures about the formal and informal sports that are now played in British parks, from Sunday football to Petanque to Skateboarding, from ballooning to orienteering. It looks at age and gender trends, and discusses the suitability of parks to respond to the new concerns with health and fitness among all sections of the population.

Working Paper 11
ISBN 1873 667 51 5

Urban Parks in Germany: Current Issues, by Ralf Ebert. This paper by one of the members of Stadtart, a cultural planning agency based in Dortmund, looks at current debates about typologies and innovations in urban parks in Germany, particularly as a result of the impact of green thinking and restoring a greater balance between town and country in the wake of de–industrialisation.

Working Paper 12
ISBN 1 873 667 61 2

The Working Papers cost £5 each (£50 the set) and can be obtained from Comedia, The Round, Bournes Green, Nr Stroud, Glos GL6 7NL. The price includes postage, but money with order is requested, payable to 'Comedia'.

BEFORE WE ARE BORN

Keith L. Moore

Recipient of the inaugural Henry Gray/Elsevier Distinguished Educator Award in 2007 — the American Association of Anatomists' highest award for excellence in human anatomy education at the medical/dental, graduate, and undergraduate levels of teaching.

American Association of Anatomists